TRUE MESSIAH

THE STORY AND WISDOM OF APOLLONIUS OF TYANA 3 BC–AD 96

Philip A. Malpas

POINT LOMA PUBLICATIONS
SAN DIEGO 1992

POINT LOMA PUBLICATIONS
P.O. Box 6507
San Diego, CA 92166

© 1990
Second printing 1992

Printed in the United States of America

Malpas, Philip A.
True Messiah
ISBN 0–913004–67–7

CONTENTS

CONTENTS

CONTENTS

ILLUSTRATIONS

PREFACE

Who and what was Apollonius of Tyana? In plain language he was the spiritual mainspring of the Century 1 "A.D." for Greece and Europe, immeasurably the greatest man of the years that covered Roman history from the days of Augustus to the death of Domitian and after. He lived from the time assigned to the birth of Jesus to A.D. 96 and a little beyond, perhaps passing the goal of a century of mortal years and living through the reigns of twelve Roman Emperors.

Why was he the greatest man of the time? Because he was the spiritual center of the western world; and as spirituality surpasses intellect more even than intellect does brute force, so his greatness surpassed that of all his contemporaries. The fact that intellect and the animal power of militarism are more spectacular and better advertised has nothing whatever to do with the matter. Nor does it matter in the least that spiritual power to very many may be a vague sort of term that means anything or nothing. If today it is not understood as a real thing, then it will be some day. Enough that there are always some who have it, and always some who understand it.

The difficulty for the historian is that a spiritual character usually loves the utmost privacy, and if some few facts of his life become public, it is somewhat rare to find anything of his personality in history. Often he is but a name, though fragments of his thought and teachings may last through the ages. Precisely this would have been the case with Apollonius had not a group of mystics under the Empress Julia Domna, wife of Septimius Severus, the Emperor so well known in Britain, gathered information about him and edited and published the diary of his Assyrian disciple, Damis. There is reason to believe that this diary or history, as edited, has a double signification, being on the one hand a plain narrative with some few rather far–fetched and seemingly absurd passages, and on the other a mystical and symbolical history in which the much–derided absurdities are often a kind of code or cipher linking the disjointed portions of the complete plan, or disguising in technically mystic language things of a nature private to the mystic and forbidden to the profane.

Indeed, there is nothing to prevent Philostratus from using the well known philosophical method of narrating historical facts with a secondary (or primary) symbolical meaning, plain to the students of his school, but to the profane, a mere 'mythical' anecdote. The method is not unknown in our own day, and if some ancient histories were read in the face of this fact, there would be found more sense in the 'fables' with which those histories are loaded.

Needless to say, this edited and abridged history, based on the translation of the Rev. Edward Berwick, is merely a narrative and a record of teachings. For the complete work, and a scholarly translation of the book by Philostratus, nothing can be better than that of Conybeare. Our own aim and purpose, and our only contri-bution, is to present the simple narrative and the philosophy that has been given to the public in a short and readable form, for the use and pleasure of those who cannot delve into the Greek and do not wish to make the task of reading the history of Apollonius too long. In these days of personality worship it may be necessary to say that the philosophy of Apollonius is the important thing, while his personality is subordinate.

As we progress in our narrative it will be convenient to give a few quotations from contemporary literature, but we find that nothing new or of import about Apollonius has hitherto been given to the public except for the valuable comments of H.P. Blavatsky. We mention her because, as students of Theosophy know, she had access to records of the school of philosophy to which Apollonius belonged, and what she says may be relied upon. In *Isis Unveiled* and in the *Theosophical Glossary* she mentions one or two inter-esting matters. (See Appendix I.)

How The Story Of Apollonius Was Written

We turn now to the year 210 A.D. The Roman Emperor, Septimius Severus, was a man well known in Britain as a soldier and governor, and his reputation for study was widespread. Quite likely he was an occult student who, as all students must, kept his researches to himself, if they are not to cease to be occult. Or, possibly, he was merely a dabbler in occult arts, such as are common enough at all times, but there is a balance in favor of his being connected with the more serious pursuit of occultism.

The popular description of such a man was quite as usual. The historian of *The Decline And Fall Of The Roman Empire* quotes it in the terms one might expect. He says that Septimius Severus was passionately addicted to the study of magic and divination, and besides the study of the interpretation of dreams and omens, was perfectly acquainted with the science of judicial astrology. What other description of his studies would be likely to pass current in the public gossip of the time?

Of the Empress, Julia Domna, it is said: "she applied herself to letters and philosophy with some success and great application; and was the patroness of every art and the friend of every man of genius."

APOLLONIUS OF TYANA

Septimius Severus had been on the throne of the Caesars since the year 194 A.D. With him the western world entered the last septenary of the "last quarter of the century" during which, we are told by H.P. Blavatsky, an effort is made to enlighten a portion of that western world with Eastern wisdom. The Eleusinian mysteries, or their shadow, still existed, but there was not very much life left in them. Queer things had been happening in Alexandria with the 'Jewish superstition.' People who ought to have known better, such as Origen and Clement, are reproached by Porphyry (i.e. 'Purple') for breaking away from their philosophy derived from Ammonius, and, as it were, selling it to Christianity, whereas Ammonius himself had been born of Christian parents and had abandoned that teaching. Persecutions had been rife and martyrdoms common at that very time. Precisely what passed for Christianity at that date would be difficult to define today. Even our histories of the period in this matter are 'arranged.'

If we let our imagination run a little we may almost perceive something in the nature of an esoteric school of philosophy at the court, Julia Domna, the learned Empress, being prominently connected with it. We may at the same time sense a counter–influence which must have attained no little force to have raised its head so high as to have taken the methods of the Neo–Platonist school of Alexandria and carried them into the opposition camp, or at any rate grafted them on to the rival traditions, as Porphyry declares. However that may be, we are not concerned with it at the moment. If our imagination is not at fault, however, we have a picture of the Empress as the central star of a galaxy of learning at the court, with a strong bias in favor of the good old philosophy, now so much corrupted with all sorts of innovations.

It might not even be going too far to suspect that her school was the lineal descendant of the famous esoteric school of philosophy which adorned and illumined Ephesus exactly a century before, when the clash and cacophony of strange doctrines was not so strident and insistent in the Empire.

2

INTRODUCTION

Already, we must suppose, the consolidating plastic mass of the new literature would be following closely the trend of the philosophies which went into its make–up of strange echoes of the mysteries, incidents in the lives of their adepts, the materializing of their allegories, the modernizing of their ancient parables, and adaptation of traditional histories to recent dates. Origen and Clement were really learned men who had drunk at the fountain of the Neo–Platonic school of Alexandria; but they had both of them thought it policy to go bodily with their learning over to the rising school of Christianity. It is quite possible that they did this at first with the idea of preserving what they could of the old philosophy in the coming storm, but it may have been cowardice, failure, desertion, ambition, or any one of the strange motives that impel even initiates of such a school to unexpected actions. The point is that they did it.

What more natural then, than that their traditions, allegories, rituals, and others of other schools should be made to act in a similar manner and be transferred to the new schools? We may look upon it as a barefaced robbery. But to them it was a merit to build these old stones in the new edifice, just as a cathedral has been injected in later centuries into the middle of the forest of columns of the mosque of Cordova. Those who did it thought it a worthy action.

The quiet school around the Empress Julia Domna could not but be aware of these little tendencies. Their system and plan were fairly safe from spoliation because they kept it to themselves, or at least disguised it in allegory and symbol, the more effective for being in outward appearance very simple and commonplace narrative and fable, though some of the deeper teachings were concealed under the strange jargon of the alchemists, as they had been for millenniums past.

Yet the signs of the coming break–up were not wanting. What could they do to meet the tidal wave that threatened to overwhelm them? Their esotericism would die out and with it their tradition, if it were not to be preserved in some outward public form. Already it was being nibbled into by the mice of the disintegrating sects that were growing up around them.

Obviously, a book must be written, half–revealing, half–concealing what they would preserve. As to the kind of book, there could be little doubt that a narrative, a biography, would be most suitable. It would arouse no great disputations nor weird interpretations, yet it could contain all they needed to say. What more appropriate than a life of the great Apollonius who had passed away precisely a century before, after a career of sanctity and purity known the world over? They had access to the diary of his Assyrian pupil and companion, Damis, and such other documents as were available. Likely enough these were among the archives of their community, but it was sufficient for the outside world to know that the learned empress "collected them." They were crude though voluminous, and needed editing. In other words, they needed arranging so as to contain within the body of the narrative and discourses the inner body of the teachings and the philosophical system. This arrangement required skill and art, and the right man was found for the purpose in Flaccus, or Flavius Philostratus, son of Verus, who had once taught rhetoric at Athens, and was known for his speeches and tracts. His eloquence was such that he was known as the 'Sophist' among the group around the Empress.

If he was not a secret Pythagorean, he knew enough of the system to do his work thoroughly. For Apollonius was a Pythagorean in the double sense that he first followed the rule of Pythagoras and then became a direct pupil of the Indian School of Philosophy to which Pythagoras had belonged as a pupil before him.

APOLLONIUS OF TYANA

THE EMPRESS JULIA DOMNA, 210 A.D.

ONE

EARLY YEARS

The pages which follow are largely based on the statements and remarks of Philostratus.

Our author begins with a note on Pythagoras and his rule of life, which was strictly followed by Apollonius.

"Though engaged in like pursuits and studies, Apollonius devoted himself to philosophy with a more divine enthusiasm, than Pythagoras," Philostratus declares, and continues:

"They who commend Pythagoras as the Samian, say of him, that before his birth in Ionia, he was Euphorbus at Troy; and that after his death at that place, which is recorded by Homer, he returned again to life. Pythagoras rejected the use of all clothing made from the skins of animals, and abstained both from eating and sacrificing them. He never polluted with blood the altars of the gods, to whom he offered cakes of honey, and frankincense, and hymns;* for such oblations he knew were more acceptable to them than whole hecatombs, and the sacrificial knife.

"He conversed with the gods, and learnt from them, how men may do what is pleasing to them, and how the contrary. Hence he spoke of the nature of things as a man inspired: for he said that other

---

*"Honey, frankincense and hymns," symbolize the essence and aroma of nature, besides having special significance in regard to the teachings of the philosophical schools. They were and are typical of a far higher spiritual education than the coarse and degrading bloodshed of less spiritual systems.

men guessed only of the divine will, but that Apollo had visited him and declared his Godhead. Pallas and the Muses, he also said, had conversed with him, without declaring who they were, as did other deities whose names and aspects were not as yet known to mortals.

"Whatever was taught by Pythagoras, was observed as a law by his disciples, who reverenced him as a man come from Jove; and the silence he enjoined was most vigilantly adhered to by them, with a zeal which a doctrine so sublime merited; for whilst it continued, they heard many things of a divine and mysterious nature, which would have been difficult for them to retain and comprehend, had they not first learnt that silence itself was the beginning and rudiment of wisdom."

There was a disciple of Apollonius, Damis the Ninevite, who wrote a diary and an account of his travels, carefully noting the opinions, discourses, and predictions of his Teacher. A person belonging to the family of Damis called the attention of the Empress Julia to these writings of the Assyrian, which until that time had not been made public.

Also, Maximus the Aegean wrote of the actions of Apollonius at Aegae. These were the books used by Philostratus. The commentaries of Damis were plain, but not eloquent, and paid no attention to style. The work of the philosopher Philostratus, was, at the bidding of the Empress, to put the information in a more literary form and style.

Apollonius was born in or about the year 3 'B.C.' at Tyana, a town of Cappadocia, founded by Greeks. He was named after his father, who belonged to an ancient family, which might be traced back to the original settlers. He was wealthy, as were many of his country men.

Shortly before his birth the Egyptian god Proteus appeared to the mother of Apollonius and announced that he himself would be her son. Proteus is the god who had a wonderful power of avoiding apprehension by transforming himself at will into anything he wished. He seemed to have foreknowledge of all things.

EARLY YEARS

Apollonius was said to have been born in a meadow, near which there stood a temple dedicated to him. His mother was told in a dream to go and gather flowers in the meadow. Her young companions amused themselves in various ways, dispersed about the place, while she fell asleep. A flock of swans, feeding in the meadow, formed a chorus round her as she slept, and beating their wings, sang in unison, while a gentle breeze fanned the air. The song of the swans awakened her suddenly and the boy was born. The people of the place said that at that instant a thunderbolt which was ready to fall on the ground rose aloft and suddenly disappeared.

When the boy grew to an age suitable for instruction, his father took him to Tarsus and left him as a pupil of Euthydemus the Phoenician, a celebrated rhetorician. Apollonius became attached to his tutor, with whom, by his father's permission, he retired to Aegae, a neighboring town, not so noisy as Tarsus, and more suitable for the study of philosophy. Here he had opportunities for meeting students of the philosophy of Plato, Chrysippus, and Aristotle, also he listened to the opinions of Epicurus without condemning them. The teachings of Pythagoras were embraced by Apollonius with the utmost zeal and enthusiasm, though his tutor knew little of that philosopher and was not particularly addicted to study of any kind. This tutor was named Euxenus, a native of Heraclea. He knew some of the sayings of Pythagoras, precisely in the manner of birds that utter phrases they are taught without understanding a word of what they say.

Apollonius in no way despised this tutor, and kept faithfully to him while in his charge, though at times he would, like the young eagle that sometimes essays a flight above its parents without seeking to leave them altogether, explore regions of philosophy beyond his tutor's reach, while submitting to his authority, and being guided by him in the ways of knowledge.

DISCIPLE OF PYTHAGORAS

But at the age of sixteen, about the year Tiberius became Emperor, Apollonius became an enthusiastic disciple of Pythagoras and a zealous admirer of his doctrine, winged thereto by a superior intelligence. None the less did he continue to respect Euxenus, and as a proof of his regard, gave him a house which his father purchased for him, with a garden and fountains belonging to it, at the same time saying: "live you in what manner you please, but for myself, I shall live after the manner of Pythagoras."

Euxenus supposed, from this declaration, that his pupil had some lofty aim in view. He asked what beginning Apollonius proposed to make for his system of life. Apollonius replied that he would begin as the physicians do, for by purifying the body they prevent disease in some and cure others.

This reply was very appropriate, since the meeting–place of young philosophers in the town of Aegae was a temple of Aesculapius, the god of medicine, who occasionally revealed himself to his devotees.

Apollonius after this ceased to eat anything that had life, declaring it to be impure and weakening to the understanding. He lived on fruits and vegetables, saying that the products of the soil alone were pure. Wine, he admitted was pure since the vine is a tree not injurious to man. Doubtless he would say this of unfermented wine, but avoided controversy as to the fermented juice of the grape by saying that he considered it adverse to a composed state of mind by reason of the power it possessed of disturbing the divine particle of spirit* of which it is formed, and therefore he abstained.

So restricting his diet, Apollonius next changed his mode of dress. He went barefoot, dressed in linen, and would have nothing to do with garments made from living creatures. He allowed his hair to grow, and spent the greater part of his time in the temple of Aesculapius.

Those who officiated in the temple were astonished at these practical applications of his philosophy, and even the God himself sometimes appeared to the priest in charge and declared that he had

---

*"The divine particle of air of which the mind is formed," is equivalent to the "divine particle of spirit." The Greek word for air and spirit is the same. The 'Holy Ghost' is the 'Holy Air' in Greek pneuma.

pleasure in performing his cures in the presence of such a witness as Apollonius.

The fame of Apollonius spread near and far, so that the Cilicians and all the residents in and about the country came to visit him. There is a proverbial saying of the Cilicians which had its origin in this circumstance, for when they see one in great haste, they say, "Whither do you run so fast? Is it to see the young man?"

Of the work of Apollonius in the temple a story is told in regard to a young Assyrian of luxurious habits who suffered from dropsy. This young man took pleasure in intoxicating liquor in spite of his sickness, and thus neglected the remedies he knew to be necessary. He slept on the couch provided for such patients, but the god gave him no dream indicating a cure. Upon the young man complaining of this the god finally appeared to him and directed him to apply to Apollonius for advice that should make him well.

He asked Apollonius what he could do for him, and the latter replied that he could restore him to health and that he was not to be blamed.

"The god," said he, "bestows health on all who are willing to receive it but you on the contrary, feed your disease. You live in total subjection to your appetite, and overload with delicacies a weak and dropsical constitution, adding clay to water."

Thus declaring clearly his opinion, Apollonius restored the Assyrian to health.

Another instance is given, also an illustration of the philosophy that lay behind the cures of Aesculapius, showing that the divine law of compensation could not be escaped, but must be fulfilled by the lawbreaker himself, neither vicarious atonement nor money being accepted from the man who remained impure at heart.

Apollonius saw one day in the temple much blood sprinkled on the altars, many sacrifices laid thereon, several Egyptian oxen and huge swine slain; in addition, there were two golden bowls filled with most precious Indian gems.

"What is the meaning of all this?" he asked the priest. "I suppose some great man is paying his respects to the deity?"

"You will be surprised to hear, I think," said the priest, "that the man has not yet even presented his petition nor has he dwelt the proper time in the temple nor has he received any benefit from the god. He has as yet received nothing; in fact, he only came yesterday, I believe, and yet he sacrifices with this extraordinary generosity. But he has promised to make more splendid and richer presents, if Aesculapius grants his petition. I hear that he is rich, and has greater possessions in Cilicia than all the rest of the Cilicians. His petition is that the god will restore him the eye he has lost."

Apollonius fixed his eyes on the ground, as was his custom, also in his old age, and asked what was the name of the man? When he heard it, he said: "I think he should not be admitted to the temple, for he is unclean, and met with the accident in a bad cause. I am of opinion that the mere circumstance of his making such costly sacrifices before the granting of his petition, proves not so much the honest sacrificer, as one who wishes to deprecate the wrath of Heaven for some enormous offense."

Aesculapius appeared by night to the priest and said: "Let both him and his offerings depart together, for he is not deserving of the eye which remains."

When the priest made inquiries concerning the supplicant, he learned that he was living scandalously. His wife had put out both the eyes of her daughter by a former husband with a needle, and one of those of her present husband, who now sought to have it restored.

In this way Apollonius showed the propriety of offering such sacrifices, and making such presents, as should not exceed the bounds of moderation. Many people flocked to the temple.

Apollonius conversed with the priest and said: "Seeing that the gods know all things, I think he who approaches them with a good conscience should pray after this wise: 'O ye Gods, grant what is convenient for me!'

"Consequently," he declared, "good things are due to the good, and the contrary to the wicked. Hence the gods, who always act rightly, send him away whom they find to be of a sound mind and free from sin, crowned not with crowns of gold, but with all manner of good things; and him whom they discover to be corrupt and polluted by vice, they give over to punishment, being the more offended with him for presuming to approach their temples conscious of his own unworthiness."

Then Apollonius turned towards Aesculapius and said: "You, Aesculapius, exercise a philosophy at once ineffable and becoming yourself, not suffering the wicked to come near the shrines, even though they bring with them the treasures of India and Sardis; and this prohibition is given from knowing that such applicants do not sacrifice and burn incense from reverence to the gods, but from the selfish motive of making atonement for their own sins, to which you will never consent, from the love you bear to justice."

Many other philosophical discourses of this kind were uttered by Apollonius whilst he was still but a youth.

IN HIS TWENTIETH YEAR

In the year 17 A.D., Apollonius being in his twentieth year, and therefore still a minor, returned to Tyana to bury his father by the side of his mother, who had died some time before. The fortune left was large, and Apollonius divided it with his elder brother, who was very dissipated and given to wine, though only twenty–three years of age; the latter had been independent of guardians since the age of twenty–one, as the law provided.

After this Apollonius returned to Aegae and changed the Temple of Aesculapius into a Lyceum and Academy, in which resounded all manner of philosophical disputation.

When he became of age and his own master, he went again to Tyana, where a friend suggested that he should endeavor to reform his elder brother. Apollonius showed a delicate modesty in recognizing the presumption of such an attempt, but declared his willingness to try, as far as lay in his power.

Very tactfully he commenced his task. First he told his brother that he himself needed little and therefore was willing to give half of his inheritance to the elder brother who needed much. In this way he secured his brother's confidence without any appearance of presuming. Gradually he led his brother to the point where he would be willing to take advice.

"Our father, who used to advise us," he said, "is dead. It now remains for us to consult each other's interest and happiness. If I do wrong in any way, I ask you to advise me, and I will correct myself; and if you should do anything wrong, I hope you will listen to my advice."

By this gentle treatment, Apollonius first made his brother willing to listen to advice, and then by degrees prevailed on him to abandon his vices, which were common enough and fashionable at the time, such as gambling, drinking, a swaggering manner, and also a foolish admiration for his hair, which he used to dye.

After this success with his brother, Apollonius tactfully did the same with his other relatives, not hesitating to give those that most needed it the remainder of his fortune, with the exception of what his own small needs demanded.

As for himself, he declared that the saying of Pythagoras that a man should have but one wife was not for him, since he had determined never to marry. By this, says Philostratus, he showed himself superior to Sophocles the Athenian, who, when old, said he had got rid of a furious master, whereas Apollonius "subdued the wild beast in his youth and triumphed over the tyrant in the vigor of his young manhood."

TWO

THE SILENCE OF APOLLONIUS

Euxenus, his former tutor, once asked Apollonius why he did not make a book of his thoughts, since he possessed such a fund of philosophical knowledge and at the same time had such a popular style of expressing himself. Apollonius replied that he had not exercised silence, and from that time forward he practiced it, as Pythagoras advised, and maintained the practice for five years. He laid a restraint upon his tongue, but read much with his eyes, and comprehended much by his understanding, committing all to memory, by the exercise of which, at the age of one hundred, "he far excelled Simonides."

The manner he used in expressing himself during his silence, had something interesting and graceful in it, for his hands and his eyes and the movements of his head made significant answers to what was said. He never appeared morose or out of spirits, and always preserved an even, placid temper. Afterwards he declared that this silence was often irksome to him, as he had many things to say which he did not say, and had to hear many disagreeable things of which he was obliged to take no notice.

In this way he passed over with a dignified silence many injurious things uttered against him.

15

APOLLONIUS OF TYANA

The years of silence were passed partly in Pamphylia and partly in Cilicia. He passed through many towns which were in an uproar with unseemly shows and vulgar spectacles, but never uttered a word of reproof with his lips. Yet by a look and the waving of his hand he caused the tumult to cease, and all those about him in the crowd were silent "as though engaged in the most mysterious ceremonies of religion." However, he took little credit for this, as he was aware that men making such tumult about mere horses and pantomimes soon become sober again, blushing and condemning themselves, whenever a man of gravity appears.

It was a different matter when, at Aspendus in Pamphylia, he was able to save the governor from being burnt alive by the populace, who meant to kill him even if he had taken refuge at the feet of the statues of the Emperor Tiberius, which being regarded as sacred ground, meant death for the violation of its sanctuary. By a gesture of his hand Apollonius asked the governor what was the matter. The latter replied that he had not wronged the people, but was a victim with them, and if not allowed to speak, must perish with the people.

Apollonius turned to the crowd and by a sign indicated that the governor must be heard. The populace were so overawed by the bearing of the philosopher that there was immediate silence and they replaced the fire they had taken from the altars in order to burn the governor.

The governor was emboldened by this to declare the exact state of the matter. The famine by which they were perishing was caused by rich men hoarding corn. He named the men who had so produced the scarcity and declared that the corn was held in secret storage in various parts of the country for sale at any price they chose to ask of famine–stricken foreigners.

The people of Aspendus, which was the third city in Pamphylia, immediately prepared to spread over the country and take the corn by force, but Apollonius signed to them not to do so, but to summon the guilty monopolists and make them consent to give the corn.

THE SILENCE OF APOLLONIUS

As soon as these arrived Apollonius was almost tempted, so sore was the distress of the people, to break his rule of silence, but he refrained. Instead, he wrote on a tablet what he wished to say, and gave it to the governor to read.

"Apollonius

"To the corn monopolists in Aspendus,

"Greeting,

The earth is the common mother of all, for she is just. You are unjust, for you have made her only the mother of yourselves: and if you will not cease from acting thus, I will not suffer you to remain upon her."

Intimidated by these words the speculators filled the market with grain, and the city recovered from its distress.

After the fulfillment of his period of silence, Apollonius went to Antioch, and entered the temple of Apollo Daphneus. Here he observed that there was no real worship performed in the temple, and that it was in the possession of barbarous people devoid of all worthy knowledge. Therefore when he spoke he retired to places more remote from the crowd, and made his abode in such temples as he found open. He declared that he sought, not the company of illiterates, but that of men.

At sunrise he performed apart from all, certain ceremonies, which he communicated only to those who had observed a silence of four years. Whenever he entered a city that happened to be of Greek origin, and was in possession of an established code of religious worship, he called the priests together, and discoursed to them concerning the nature of their Gods; and if he found that they had departed from their customary ritual, he always set them right. But when he came to a city whose religious rites and customs were barbarous, and different from others, he inquired by whom they were established, and for what they were intended, and afterwards in what manner they were observed, at the same time suggesting whatever occurred to him as better and more becoming.

Next, he visited his followers, commanding them to ask what they pleased, saying that they who cultivated philosophy in the

17

manner he enjoined, should in the morning converse with the gods, at midday concerning the gods, and in the evening of human affairs. When he had answered all the questions put forward by his friends, and talked as much as he thought sufficient, he addressed the multitude, with whom he discoursed in the evening, but never before noon.

When he had finished speaking he had himself anointed and rubbed, afterwards plunging into a cold bath, declaring that hot baths were the old age of men. To the people of Antioch who, for their crimes, were forbidden the use of the hot baths, he said that the Emperor had given them long life for their wickedness. At one time certain Ephesians were about to stone the master of the baths for not making them hot enough and Apollonius said:

"You blame the master of the baths for your not bathing to your satisfaction, but I blame you for bathing at all!"

The manner of Apollonius's speech was not elevated, nor inflated with the language of poetry, nor yet too refined, nor too Attic; he considered speech that exceeded the ordinary level of the Attic to be dissonant and unpleasant. He employed no fastidious nicety in the division of his discourses, nor did he use fine–spun sentences; nor was he ever known to adopt an ironical manner, nor any kind of apostrophizing with his listeners.

Now the tripod is the emblem of truthful speech; it is dedicated to Apollo, the god of true oracles, and to Bacchus. It is the seat on which the inspired sibyls sat when delivering oracles when possessed by the god of that oracle.

Philostratus says of Apollonius: "He spoke as it were from a tripod"; for example: "I know," and "It seems to me," and "To what purpose is this," and "You must know." His sentences were short and adamantine, his words authoritative and adapted to the sense, and the bare utterance of them conveyed a tone as though they were sanctioned by the scepter of royalty.

He was once asked by a subtle debater why he did not declare what side of a question he proposed to take in an argument. He replied: "When I was a young man, I used to do that; but now it is no longer necessary, for it is my duty to teach the result of my investigations, and not to investigate any longer."

When asked by the same logician how a wise man should speak, he replied: "As a legislator. For it is the part of a legislator to command the multitude to do what he himself is convinced ought to be done."

(By such sentences Apollonius indicated that he had attained the degree of a master of philosophy, and had ceased to be a mere student.)

"In this way he conducted himself at Antioch, and converted many who were strangers to all knowledge."

THREE

TRAVELS

Apollonius determined to visit India and the wise men of that country who were called Brachmanes, and Germanes,* saying it was the business of young men to travel and make themselves known in foreign countries. To converse with the magi at Babylon and Susa, and to learn all they knew, he considered would be in itself sufficient reason for undertaking the journey.

He declared his intentions to his companions, who were seven in number, but they disagreed with him and endeavored to dissuade him from his purpose.

Then he said to them: "I have consulted the gods, and I declared their will to you, to make trial of your courage, whether you will go with me or not. Since I find you are not resolute enough to go, I bid you farewell, and desire you may study philosophy. It is my duty to go where wisdom and my Genius [*daimon*] lead me."

---

* Brachmanes were, strictly speaking, Buddhist. The ancient basic teachings of the Brâhmins seems to have been pure Buddhism as it was ages before Gautama the Buddha restored it. See *Isis Unveiled*, vol. II chap. vii. The Germanes were said to be Indian philosophers (generally called Gymnosophist, though not all of them were naked philosophers or yogis, as that term would denote), who lived alone in the forests, abstaining from wine and married life, and practicing many austerities. We call a man a 'gymnast,' although he may not be naked; similarly the word 'gymnosophist' is not always restricted to its primitive sense.

After this, he departed from Antioch, attended only by two domestics of his own family. These were expert scribes, the one eminent for the dispatch with which he wrote, (probably a short-hand writer such as Cicero and others employed), and the other for the beauty of his handwriting.

THE MEETING WITH DAMIS

At the ancient Nineveh, Apollonius met with Damis the Assyrian, who became his companion and disciple, and from whose memoirs, written as a diary, the main part of the present work is extracted. "Let us go together," said Damis. "God shall be your guide, and you shall be mine."

Damis further declared that his knowledge of the way to Babylon and his acquaintance with the languages of the Armenians, Medes, Persians, and Cadusians, would be useful.

"My friend, I know them all myself, though I never learnt them," said Apollonius, to the amazement of Damis, though it was years before the latter began to understand the full significance of the statement. "Be not astonished," continued Apollonius, "at my knowing all languages, for I know the very thoughts of men, even what they do not utter."

When Damis heard this, he adored him, considering him as one inspired (Daimon). He then became a proselyte to the teachings of Apollonius and what he learned he did not forget.

Philostratus remarks: "This Assyrian had some eloquence, though ignorant of elegant writing. Yet his observation of whatever was said or done in company was acute, and he kept an exact account of all that passed, which appears from a book he wrote called the *Apolloniana.*"

So minute and trifling were the details that were sometimes recorded that a wit declared in a derogatory tone that the crumbs collected put him in mind of the scraps eaten by the dogs which snap up whatever falls from their master's table.

Damis replied simply: "If the gods have feasts, and eat at them, they also have attendants who wait on them, and whose business it is to see that none of the ambrosia be lost."

Such was the companion and friend by whom Apollonius was accompanied during a great part of his life.

When Apollonius passed into Mesopotamia, the customs officer at the bridge of Zeugma asked what baggage he had with him. The traveler replied that he brought Temperance, Justice, Continence, Fortitude, Patience, and many other virtues (all of them having feminine names). The collector of customs wrote down the names and said he had "made a note of the names of the maids."

"They are not maids," said Apollonius. "They are my mistresses, who travel with me! [This little jeu d'esprit has value in explaining how in some philosophical legends, strict ascetics are said to have a number of wives.]

In Mesopotamia there dwelt nomad tribes of Arabs and Armenians, among whom Apollonius learned the Arabian art of understanding the language of animals. Divination by birds among this people is as much respected as that by oracles.

"This talent is obtained according to some," says Philostratus in his symbolical language, "by their feeding on the heart, and according to others, on the liver of dragons."

After passing beyond Ctesiphon, Apollonius entered the territories of Babylon. The King, Bardanes Arsacida, was not fully settled on the throne, and all new arrivals in the country were carefully examined by the military guards, who suspected everyone. Apollonius was taken before the viceroy, or satrap, who was then taking the air in his palanquin. As soon as he saw the gaunt, linen–clad figure of the philosopher, he screamed out in fright like a woman. Finally, when his courage revived, he looked up and asked: "Whence art thou sent to us?"

"From myself!" said Apollonius. "I am come to teach you to be men, in spite of yourselves."

"Who are you, that you dare to enter the King's dominions? asked the Satrap, becoming bolder.

"The whole world is mine, and I have leave to go wherever I please through it!" answered Apollonius.

"Answer me properly, or I will have you tortured!" said the Satrap.,

"Oh! that the punishment were to be inflicted by your own hands, that you might pay the merited penalty for daring to touch such a man!" said Apollonius, boldly declaring the philosophical law that every man must pay for his own deeds.

That eunuch was astonished at the stranger's wonderful familiarity with the language. He changed his tone and adjured Apollonius in the name of the gods, to say who he was.

"Since you condescend to ask me so courteously, I will tell you," said the Greek philosopher. "I am Apollonius of Tyana, going to the King of the Indians to learn from him what is happening in that country. I shall be glad to see the King, for he is reputed to be not without virtue, if it is Bardanes who has just regained his kingdom."

"He is the man, divine Apollonius," replied the Satrap (for of you we have heard long ago). "He is one who would resign his crown to a wise man, and he will take care to have you and your companions provided with camels for your journey to India. For my part I make you my guest."

Upon this, the bewildered Satrap offered him heaps of gold, to help himself, but Apollonius firmly refused to touch it. He offered wine of Babylon such as the King gives to his ten viceroys or satraps; he offered roasted pork and goat–flesh; bread and meal, and all he could think of as being desirable for the philosopher's journey. Then he suddenly remembered who it was he was addressing, and was mightily confused, for he could hardly offer a greater insult than wine and flesh to such a man.

But Apollonius showed no resentment. "You will be treating me sumptuously if you give me bread and vegetables," he said.

"You shall have leavened bread, and great dates that look like amber for their richness; vegetables you shall have from the river gardens of the Tigris."

"I prefer the vegetables that grow wild by themselves to those that are forced and artificially cultivated," he said, "for I think they are sweeter to the taste."

"I fear not," said the Satrap. "The soil about Babylon abounds in wormwood and tends to make the vegetables bitter and disagreeable."

Apollonius took leave of the Satrap with all the respect due to his office, but gently rebuked him for his uncivil reception, by his parting remark: "Cease not from doing good, but I say also, begin by doing good."

In their subsequent journey they came upon a lioness that had just been killed by the huntsmen, who were amazed at her size and the extraordinary fact that there were no less than eight half–formed cubs. From this omen, Apollonius deduced the fact that their stay with the King would last just a year and eight months. He used the occasion to give Damis an opportunity of deducing an interpretation from the circumstance, before declaring the correct augury.

When approaching Cissia after entering the province of Babylon, Apollonius had the following vision in his sleep "prepared by the deity who communicated it." He saw some fishes cast on the shore and panting for breath. They complained like mortals and bewailed the element they had lost. They looked as if imploring the aid of a dolphin who was swimming near them, and seemed as much to be pitied as men in exile, deploring their hard fortune.

Apollonius considered the interpretation of the vision, but gave Damis the opportunity to explain it as best he could, before telling him what it meant. Damis was alarmed and almost ready to turn back at the suggestion that they were like "fish out of water" in a foreign land. Apollonius laughed at him, telling him he was not yet a philosopher, to be alarmed at the dream. Then he declared the purport.

The district of Cissia was inhabited by an isolated group of Eretrians exiled from Greece by Darius five hundred years before, like fishes taken in a net. The gods seemed to command Apollonius to take all the care he could of them, "for peradventure the souls of the Greeks, who were cast by fate on this land, have invited me hither for their benefit."

Apollonius did all he could for the dead and the living. He enclosed the graves and restored the tombs, he offered libations, and made sacrifices without victims or the shedding of blood. This was more than had ever had been done for those who had exiled them, for these died unburied about the Greek island whence they had come, ten years later. For the living, Apollonius in his very first audience with the King obtained the sole use and enjoyment of their hill, the only fertile part of their land, for them forever, by royal grant. This was a very important concession, as they had hitherto suffered from the annual raids of the nomads, and desert tribes who left them little of the fruit of their industry.

Damis says that Apollonius had several conversations with the Babylonian Magi either at midday or midnight, but he was never permitted to be present at these interviews. Being asked his opinion of the Magi, Apollonius said: "They are wise, but not in all things."

The manner of his entry into Babylon was unusual. He bore no presents for the King and he merely gave a philosophical reply to the demand that he, like all strangers, should worship the golden image of the King as he entered. The only exception made was in the case of Roman ambassadors. On the presentation to him of the King's golden image, he asked: "Whose image is this?"

They told him it was the King.

"If this man whom you worship is so fortunate as to be praised by me for his virtue and goodness," said Apollonius, "he will have honor enough." And he passed through the gates.

The Satrap was astonished at such behavior and at his appearance. He noted his name, country, occupation, appearance, and the reason for his journey, on the official tablets and caused Apollonius to be detained while he reported the matter to the 'King's Ears'–the agents of the court whose business it was to guard against all possibility of action against the throne.

These officials sent for him, ordering that he should not be molested in any way. "Why do you despise the King?" they asked.

25

"I do not despise him," was the reply.

"But you will do so later on?" they asked again.

"Certainly I shall, if I find by conversing with him that he is not as good and virtuous as I expect."

"What presents do you bring him?" they inquired.

"I bring fortitude and justice, and some other like virtues," said the amazing stranger.

"How is this?" asked the King's office. "Do you bring these presents from an idea that our King has not such virtues already?"

"Not exactly that," said Apollonius " But I suppose that if he has time already, I can teach him to use them."

"Yet it is by the very exercise of these virtues that our King has regained his lost kingdom, and recovered his palace, not without much labor and toil."

"How many years ago did he do that?" asked the philosopher. "Two years and two months," replied the King's minister.

Then Apollonius's manner grew intensely forcible, as he used the formula with which he emphasized his weightier sayings.

"O thou guardian of the royal person, or any other appellation if it please thee better, *hearken to what I say:* Darius, the father of Cyrus and Artaxerxes, after a reign of about sixty years, when he found his end approaching, is said to have sacrificed to justice, exclaiming, *O mistress, whosoever thou art.* From this it is fair to assume that he loved justice all his life, though he knew her not, nor ever thought himself possessed of her. Thus it was that he educated his children so foolishly that they warred one against the other; one was wounded and the other killed by his brother. Now you praise beyond all deserving a King, as if possessed of every virtue, who perhaps does not know how to maintain his throne. Yet, if he becomes better than he is, the gain will be yours and not mine."

One of the Babylonians looking at him declared: "Without a doubt the gods have sent this extraordinary man to us. I am of opinion that men of virtue conversing with a prince so well instructed as our king must make him wiser and better, and more gracious, inasmuch as these virtues are painted in his countenance."

TRAVELS

Then all ran to the palace, proclaiming the good tidings of a man being at the King's gates, who was *wise,* and a *Greek,* and *an excellent counselor.*

FOUR

WITH THE MAGI

The King was offering sacrifice in the presence of the Magi when the news of Apollonius's arrival was brought to him. He immediately recalled a dream he had dreamed the day before, that he was Artaxerxes the son of Xerxes, and that his face became like that of the latter. The interpretation was plain. For Themistocles had come from Greece to Artaxerxes and by his conversation had made him estimable, as his father had been; also he had justified his own reputation as a Greek philosopher. Obviously, Apollonius would benefit him as Themistocles had benefited Artaxerxes, and would prove to be as great a philosopher as his reputation declared.

Apollonius passed throughout the gorgeous palace in amiable discussion with Damis as to various questions of Greek mystic, without paying the slightest attention to the sumptuous splendor of the building. The palace court was large, and the King called aloud to him from a distance and bade him join in the sacrifice to the sun of a white horse from the Nisean plains.

"Do you, O King, sacrifice after your manner," said Apollonius, "but allow me to sacrifice after my own fashion." So saying, he took the incense in his hand and said, "O Sun, conduct me to whatever part of the world may seem good to you and me; and grant me to know only the virtuous; as to the wicked, I wish neither to

28

know them nor be known by them." Then he cast the incense on the fire, observing the smoke, how it rose and curled and shot into spiral forms. Afterwards he touched the fire as though the omens were favorable, and said: "O King, do you continue to sacrifice after the ceremonies of your own country; for my part, I have observed what belongs to mine."

He then withdrew from the sacrifice lest he should be made an accomplice in the shedding of blood.

Apollonius was glad to find the king spoke Greek as though it were his mother–tongue, so that they could converse the more freely. The faculty that Apollonius possessed of speaking all languages was not always drawn upon. He told the king of his intended visit to the Indians and that he was anxious to know the wisdom of the Magi at the court, whether they were really wise in religious matters or not. He declared his own system of philosophy to be that of Pythagoras the Samian, who taught him to worship the gods in the way he had demonstrated, "to discern their several natures, and respect them accordingly, to converse with them and dress myself in garments made from the genuine fleece of the earth, not torn from the sheep, but from what grows pure from the pure, from linen, the simple produce of earth and water. I let my hair grow, and abstain from all animal food, in obedience to the doctrine of Pythagoras. With you or any other man, I can never indulge in the gratifications of the table. I promise to free you from perplexing and vexatious cares, for I not only know, but foreknow what is to be."

Realizing the absolute sincerity of Apollonius, the king declared that he was more pleased at his arrival than if he had the wealth of India and Persia added to his own. The Greek should be the royal guest and have apartments in the royal palace.

"If you should visit Tyana, my birthplace," asked Apollonius, "and if I should offer you lodging in my house, would you accept?"

"Hardly that," said the king, "unless your house were large enough to receive me and my attendants and in a way becoming my rank and consequence."

"Then," said Apollonius, "I should be no more comfortable than you, if I were to live in a house above my condition of life. All excess is troublesome to the wise, as the want of it is to the great ones of the earth, such as yourself. Therefore I would prefer to lodge with some private individual, of like fortune with myself. But as for conversation, I will converse with you as much as you please."

The king respected his feelings and assented. Apollonius lodged with a Babylonian who was a man of good family and character.

While they were at supper a eunuch arrived from the king with a message. "The king gives you the choice of ten boons, and permission to choose them yourself. He insists that you should ask nothing of mean value or little worth, but he is anxious to impress you and ourselves with a sense of his great bounty."

"When is the choice to be made?" asked Apollonius.

"Tomorrow," replied the messenger, as he went off to summon the king's relatives and friends to witness the respect paid to so honored a supplicant.

Apollonius appeared to be considering the things he might ask, which was somewhat puzzling to Damis, who, knowing his friend and teacher, almost expected him to ask for nothing. A man whose prayers to the gods were usually after the formula, *"Ye gods, grant me few possessions and no wants!"* would surely ask little of the king.

While in this state of curiosity, Appollonius took the opportunity of pointing out that before a day was past they would have an example of the fact that the forcible destruction of the means of sinning physically had no effect on the mind, and that such practices were worse than useless. He was thinking of the king's messenger. As a master-philosopher often does, he pretended to be a little ignorant of life as it is in reality, and let Damis pulverize his theories with blunt statements of 'fact,' such as that when deprived of the means of sinning by physical means a man could not sin. By so doing Damis only succeeded in being caught by the admission that he needed the lesson when it came. His hasty remark that a child

30

would know what he said to be true, as though he wondered at his master's ignorance of practical life, recoiled on his own head next day. The conversation led to a consideration of the banishment of desire from the mind, which is just what Appolonius was quietly leading up to.

"The virtue of temperance," declared Appollonius, "consists in not yielding to passion though you feel all the incentives to it, but in abstaining from it and showing yourself superior to all its allurements."

Damis missed the point altogether, not realizing that the desire of the body and the desire of money are really only different facets of the same quality of desire.

"Let us talk about that later on," he said. "Meanwhile you have to think of the royal message so nobly given. I think personally you will ask for nothing, but the question is how to do so without seeming to slight the king's offer. Remember where we are in the king's power, and how we must avoid even the appearance of treating the king with disrespect. Besides, we have enough money to get to India, but not enough to return, so it is necessary to consider carefully what to do."

The tone of the disciple who 'knows better' is plainly discernible. Was it ever otherwise? Apollonius was enjoying the joke, which was serious enough, for he had to teach Damis without appearing to do more than 'draw him out'– precisely the meaning of the word 'education.'

With the serious face of an unpractical theorist he did just the last thing Damis expected him to do. He almost pleaded for the right to take money from anyone in his character of a philospher. Why, the very test of a true teacher is that he will accept never a penny for his teachings and despises money that comes in a personal guise. He quoted philospher after philospher who had sought money, until Damis began to wonder what had happened to him. Then to drive the lesson home by sudden contrast, Apollonius told him that nothing was so unpardonable to a wise man as the love of money. All other things may be forgiven him of men, but not this, since the display of a love of money will naturally cause it to be supposed that he is already overcome by the love of good living, fine clothes, wine, etc.

"If you think that committing a fault at Babylon is not the same as committing one at Athens, Damis, remember that *every place is Greece to a wise man*. He esteems no place desert or barbarous whilst he lives under the eyes of virtue, whose regards are extended to very few men, and looks on such with a hundred eyes. Surely an athlete who has to contend at Olynthos, or in Macedonia, or in Egypt, will train himself just as much as he would when contending among the Greeks, and in their most celebrated places of exercise?"

Damis was ashamed of his hasty arguments and asked pardon for having presumed to give such advice.

"Be not troubled, Damis," said his teacher. "I have not spoken for the sake of rebuke, but for the purpose of illustration."

The eunuch came to summon Apollonius to the king for the ceremony of the granting of the boons. The latter stayed to perform his accustomed religious duties and then went to the king. All the court were amazed at his singular and venerable appearance. The king promptly offered him ten great boons to be chosen by himself.

"I will not refuse," said Apollonius, "but there is one above all that I value more than many tens." He then told the unhappy history of the exiled Eretrians, and pleaded that they might remain in possession of the hill granted them by Darius.

The king declared that they had been enemies; they had taken up arms against their rulers and had been almost exterminated. But now they should be considered friends and given a just governor over them. "But why not accept the remaining nine boons?" asked the king in some little surprise that this was all Apollonius required of him.

"Because I have not had time to make more friends," said the philosopher, ever thinking of the welfare of the others and indifferent to his own.

"But surely you have needs of your own?" asked the king. "Is there nothing you require for yourself?"

"Nothing but a little fruit and bread," replied Apollonius. "They make an excellent meal!"

During this extraordinary scene very conclusive evidence indeed arrived that a man physically deprived of the power of sinning could and did retain the same power mentally with undiminished force. One of the eunuchs was discovered in the king's chamber where he had been expressly forbidden to go, as he had been forbidden to join the others of his class when they were dressing the king's wives.

So great was the offense that the king appealed to Apollonius to declare a fitting sentence for the wretch. Death many times over was a mild punishment according to the notions of the time.

"Let him go free!" said Apollonius. "That is my sentence."

The king and court were overwhelmed with amazement at this strange decision.

"It is not a pardon, but a punishment," said Apollonius. "Let him live, and he will suffer from his diseased mind, gaining no pleasure from eating, or drinking, or amusements, or sleeping; spending his life in imagining impossibilities; he will be so miserable that he will wish you had put him to death now. He will plead for death, and if you do not give it he will put an end to his own existence."

In this manner Apollonius demonstrated the power of the law which is more just than all the laws of men, and unerring in its power to balance cause and effect. At the same time the king, by remitting the death penalty, himself escaped the operation of the same law which would have held him accountable for taking the life of another. This is the philosophical law known as Karma, the law of action and reaction, which are equal and inevitable.

Invited to go hunting, Apollonius declined, since it was no more pleasing to give pain and suffering to animals and confine them in captivity than it was to sacrifice them.

Asked the best way of reigning in security, he replied: "By honoring many and trusting few."

He pointed out the folly of engaging in wars of small matters which, if evil or unjust, were infinitely less so than the evils and injustices of war against so great a power as that of the Romans.

The king, being sick to death, was visited by Apollonius, who discoursed on the nature of the soul so eloquently that the king revived.

"Apollonius not only made me despise my kingdom, but death itself!" he declared.

The king one day boasted of having spent two whole days in hearing one cause in his administration of justice, so great was his desire to do right.

"I am sorry you took so long to find out what is just!" was all the satisfaction he received from the philosopher.

Displaying his enormous wealth, the king was told by Apollonius: "You look upon it as so much wealth, but I regard it as so much straw." "How then am I to deal with it?" asked the King.

"By making a proper use of it, for you are a king," said Apollonius. In this he declared his doctrine of wealth being but a trust held for the account of all.

Privately to Damis Apollonius remarked one day that the king was a courteous prince, too good to reign over barbarians. Evidently the little surprising replies he sometimes made to the king were not regarded nor meant as rebukes but, as Damis himself had been told, 'illustrations.' The time for departure having arrived according to the omen which had declared they should be twenty months at Babylon, Apollonius prepared to leave his willing host. He recalled the nine ungranted boons, and asked the king if he might not now claim one more.

"Thou best of princes, I have shown no mark whatever of favor to my host with whom I have been living, and I am also under many obligations to the Magi. I beg of you to respect them for my sake, for they are wise men, greatly devoted to your service."

The king was delighted with this unselfish request.

"Tomorrow," he said, "you shall see these men made objects of emulation, and highly rewarded. And more than that, though you yourself will take nothing, at least let some of those men with Damis accept some part of my wealth, as much as ever they wish."

As soon as they heard this, they all turned away, and Apollonius said to the king as he pointed to them: "You see my hands, though many, are all alike!" This is the true philosophical symbol of the teacher and his disciples, and shows a quiet way Apollonius had of inclucating his philosophy.

But the way to India over the Caucasus is through a three days' desert, and the king provided camels and water and provisions. The inhabitants of the Caucasus—country, he declared, were hospitable and would receive him well.

"But what present will you bring me when you return?" asked the king.

"A most acceptable gift," said Apollonius. "If I become wiser by the conversation of the men of that country, I shall return to you better than I leave you."

The king embraced him. "Go thy way," he said, "for the gift will be great."

FIVE

APOLLONIUS IN INDIA

In passing over the Caucasus (Hindu Kush?) Apollonius by a conversation with Damis declares the true road of philosophy. By making his first questions seem absurd and then point by point showing their inner meaning, he makes the lesson more easily remembered. Discoursing on the beauty of the mountain landscape, Apollonius asked Damis whether he thought that the previous day's journey in the valley was really on a lower level than their present lofty path.

"Of course it was, unless I have lost my reason," replied Damis.

"How do the two paths differ, then? In what lies the advantage of today?" asked the Master.

"Today's journey has been made by but few, while yesterday's was through a country frequented by many travelers besides ourselves."

"Yet one may live far from the noise of men and in places frequented by few, even in a city," said Apollonius.

"I meant more than that," said Damis. "Yesterday we passed through populous villages, but today through regions untrodden by human foot; regions esteemed divine and holy. Even the barbarians, says our guide, call them the dwellings of the gods." Saying which he lifted up his eyes to the lofty summit of the mountain above them.

APOLLONIUS IN INDIA

Apollonius asked him: "What knowledge of the divine nature have you acquired by being nearer to heaven?"

"None at all. What I knew yesterday of the divine nature, that I know today, without any addition at all."

"Then you are still Below and have learnt nothing by being Above, and my question in not so absurd as it looked at first."

"I acknowledge I had some vague idea that I should be wiser than when we ascended, on coming down," said Damis. "I have heard of various philosophers who made their celestial observations on eminences and lofty mountains, but I fear that I shall not know more even if I ascend mountains higher than any of them."

"Nor did they so learn more," said Apollonius, "no more than any goat–keeper or shepherd who sees the heavens from the hill–tops. But in what manner a supreme Being superintends the human race, and how he would be worshiped, the nature of virtue, justice, and temperance, neither will Mount Athos show to those who climb its summit, nor hymned Olympus, if the soul does not make such studies the object of its contemplation. But if it does engage in such topics pure and undefiled, I tell you that it will rise far above Caucasus itself."

So they traveled, Master and Disciple, over the mighty peaks and passes of Caucasus, where the drama of the world and chained Prometheus left so deep an impression on the unlearned dwellers of the plain that they showed the bolts in the mountain-side, where the mighty titan had been held in bonds that humanity might rise to heights "Above" all the cloud–capped peaks of earth "Below," while yet engaged in daily duty truly done. For that is true philosophy.

When they met a tribe of wandering Arabs who received them with pleasure and gave them wine and honey and lion–meat, Apollonius told Damis of the use of meat and wine drinking. They rejected the meat, but Damis took the date–spirit and prepared to drink, pouring out the usual libation to God the Savior, Jupiter Salvator.

Damis was so unversed as yet in the spirit of his master's teachings (he had not known him long) that he offered some of the date-wine to Apollonius himself, saying it was not the product of the vine, therefore need not be refused. Apollonius tried to bring the Assyrian's mind to realize that the material was nothing, but the spirit everything; that the love of money does not cease to be love of money because the thing desired may be coin of another metal or country than the Greek, or money's worth; that the insult to the soul of intoxicating liquor is not lessened because it comes from another tree than the vine.

"Besides, you do in reality look upon it as wine, for you have made the usual libation to Jupiter. But what I say is in my own defense and not a rebuke to you. I do not prohibit you or your companions from drinking it. Even more, so little do I see that you have profited by the abstention from eating meat that I give you permission to eat it. I see the abstention from meat has profited you nothing at all. As to myself, I find it suitable to me in the practice of that philosophy to which I have devoted myself from my youth."

So gently did the great philosopher declare the matter that Damis, who had not seen the grain within the husk, was pleased at the permission given to eat and drink with his companions. He had approached the mountain, but his mind was still Below, far below.

The sight of elephants aroused much interest and discussion. The work in life of Apollonius was to practice philosophy and to teach it to those willing to learn. Therefore he draws moral lessons from the natural history of these wonderful animals, so gently as not to offend by seeming to preach to one who was not strong enough of character to take his wisdom neat, as one may say.

The Master leads Damis to considering the wonder of an animal as powerful as a living fortress being guided by a little Indian child not big enough to bear a spear or shield. Damis confesses it is so wonderful to him that he would buy the boy if he could, for if he could rule an elephant, surely he could rule a large household even better. Yes, he would put him in charge of racehorses, but not a warhorse, because the little fellow could not carry the armor. Not a doubt of it, the boy was one of the most wonderful children in the world!

Not so, declared the Master. It is the elephant that is wonderful, because he possess such self–control as to govern himself, for love of the boy. "Of all creatures the elephant is the most docile, and when once accustomed to submit to man he bears all things from him; he conforms to his taste, and loves to be fed out of his hand like a favorite dog. When his keeper comes you will see him fawning upon him with his trunk, and letting him put his head into his mouth, which he keeps open as long as is desired. This we saw practiced among the Nomads. Yet at night he is said to bewail his servitude, not with a loud noise, as at other times, but with a low and piteous murmur. And if a man happens to surprise him in his situation, he restrains his sorrow, as if he were ashamed. Therefore it is the elephant which governs himself, and the best of his own docile nature, which influences his conduct more than the boy on his back who seems to manage him."

Damis records this conversation, and Philostratus publishes it. The discourse of Apollonius is so full of wonderful lessons that it seems a pity that there is no indication whether Damis saw the application or not. However, as the teachings of the Indian school of philosophy which Pythagoras practiced are not unknown, we can see the drift of much that may have appeared to many little more than philosophic chatter. In this simple talk about elephants, which it seems Apollonius knew better than his disciple, though they had both seen them for the first time on this journey, Apollonius is using an exoteric illustration to portray the doctrines of universal brotherhood including all that lives and breaths and not only mankind; also the life of the philosopher who submits himself to the laws of nature of his own free will, and not as a slave to a master, doing his duty in his present position until he grows out of those circumstances in course of time, the wiser for the experience. So many of these conversations show the method; the situation is put colorlessly before the pupil, and if he is wise, his intuition will show him the application, to be followed or not as he pleases; the Teacher never forces him at all, one way or the other, and often conceals propositions of immense importance beneath a seemingly trivial conversational exterior.

As Philostratus says: "Many philosophical discourses they had together of this kind, most of which were taken from such occurrences of the day as deserved to be noticed."

In other words—the words of the Indian School of Philosophy— "Life is the Great Teacher."

On arrival at the Indus, they asked their Babylonian guide if he knew about the crossing. He said he had never passed over and therefore did not know whether it was fordable or not.

"Then why did you not provide yourself with a guide?" they asked him.

"Because I have one here that will direct you," he said as he produced a letter written by Bardanes. This mark of kindly thoughtfulness on the part of their host was much appreciated. He reminded the Indian Governor of the Indus of former favors which he had never desired should be recompensed; it was not his custom to expect requital for favors done. But if he would treat Apollonius well, and convey him wherever he desired, the debt would not be forgotten. Also the guide had been given gold, that there might be no necessity to apply for help to strangers.

On receiving the letter, the Indian Governor expressed himself as valuing it highly, and promised to treat Apollonius as though he had been recommended by no less a person than the king of the Indians himself. The royal barge was placed at his disposal, with ferries for the camels and guides for the country of the Hydraotes. The Governor provided him in addition with a letter to his own sovereign, entreating him to this Greek, this divine man, with the same respect as he had been treated by Bardanes.

APOLLONIUS IN INDIA

KING PHRAOTES

The king invited Apollonius to be his guest for three days, as the laws of the country did not allow strangers to remain longer than that time in the city. The Greek philosopher was then conducted to the palace by the messengers and the interpreter sent by the king.

No pomp or pageantry was visible in the palace; no spearmen or lifeguards appeared; there were merely a few domestics, such as are usual in any good house, and not more than three or four persons in waiting who had constant access to the king. Apollonius was more pleased with the simplicity that reigned throughout the palace than with all the proud magnificence of Babylon. He judged the king to be a philosopher.

Through the interpreter, Apollonius addressed the king: "I am happy to see you study philosophy!"

"And I," replied the king, "am equally happy that you think so."

"Is the moderation I see established everywhere the effect of the laws or is it produced by yourself?" asked the Greek.

"The laws," said the king, "prescribed moderation. But I carry my idea of it beyond the letter, and even the spirit of the laws. I am rich, and I want little. Whatever I possess more than is necessary for my own use, is considered as belonging to my friends."

"Happy are you," said Apollonius, "in being possessed of such a treasure, and in preferring friends from whom are derived so many blessings, to gold and silver."

"But it is my enemies," replied the king, "on whom I bestow my riches. By their means I keep the neighboring barbarians in subjection. Formerly these used to infest my kingdom, but now, instead of making raids on my territories, they keep others from doing so."

Apollonius asked, with reference to the great Indian King conquered by Alexander nearly four hundred years before, if Porus was accustomed to send them presents.

"Porus loved war, but I love peace," was the king's answer.

So delighted was Apollonius with this reply that when in later times he rebuked one Euphrates for not behaving like a true philosopher, he said "Let us reverence Phraotes."

A provincial governor was desirous to crown Phraotes with a rich diadem in token of his great obligations towards his benefactor. The king refused. "Even if I admired such things, I would cast it from me in the presence of Apollonius," he said. "To wear ornaments to which I am not accustomed would show an ignorance of my guest and a forgetfulness of what is due to myself."

As to diet, the king informed Apollonius that he drank no more wine than he used in his libations to the sun. Satisfied with the exercise alone, he gave all the game he killed in hunting to his friends, and was himself well content with vegetables, the pith and fruit of the palm-tree, and the produce of a well-watered garden. In addition, he had many dishes from trees he cultivated with his own hands.

Never forgetful of his duty in preparing Damis for a life of true philosophy, Apollonius cast many a glance at Damis while the king spoke, showing his pleasure at the recital of such moderation of life in eating and drinking, and doubtless hoping that his disciple would appreciate the indirect lesson in the "Science of life" which is true philosophy.

After settling everything relative to the journey to the "Brachmanes" (Buddhist philosophers and adepts), seeing the Babylonian guide well looked after, and the guide from the Governor of the Indus on his homeward way, the king, taking Apollonius by the hand, told the interpreter he might depart. Then in Greek he asked Apollonius, "Will you make me your guest?"

"Why did you not speak to me in Greek at first," asked Apollonius, in some astonishment.

"Because I might have appeared too presuming, either from not knowing myself, or from not remembering that it has pleased fortune to make me a non-Greek. But now, overcome by the love I have for you and the pleasure you seem to take in my company, I can no longer conceal myself. I will give you many proofs of my acquaintance with the Greek tongue."

"Then why do you not invite me to be your guest, rather than ask me to make you mine?"

"Because I regard you as my superior in virtue; for of all gifts a prince can possess, I deem wisdom the brightest." When he had said this, the king took Apollonius and his companion to his own bath. This was a garden, about five hundred feet long, in the middle of which was a tank fed by cool and refreshing streams. Running-paths were on both sides of the pool, and here the king often exercised with discus and javelin after the Greek fashion. A young man of twenty-seven years, he was of a sound and robust constitution, much given to physical exercise. Afterwards he would plunge into the bath and amuse himself with swimming. After the bath they went to the royal banquet, crowned with flowers, as was the custom whenever the Indians were invited to the feast in the king's palace.

The manner of dining is described: the king reclining with not more than five of his relatives in his company, and the rest of the party seated round the central large table, to which they go and help themselves as they need. Jugglers amuse them, such as the boy who leaps from a height at the moment that a very sharp javelin is thrown upward from below. So well calculated is the aim and the leap that he only misses falling on the point by a somersault which appears to keep him suspended in the air, for a moment almost touching the point of the spear. Then there was the man who would hit a hair with the sling, so accurate was his aim. Also the acrobat who would outline his son with javelins as he stood stiffly against a board, without wounding him.

Damis and his companions were vastly taken with the skill of the acrobats, but Apollonius, who had a seat among the king's relatives at his own table, took little notice of these circus tricks. He asked the king how he had learnt the Greek language and philosophy, as he supposed there would not be any teachers in that part of the world.

The king smiled at the philosopher's persistence in questioning all as to whether they were philosophers, just as his ancestors used to ask every arrival by sea if he were a pirate, so common was the practice of that great crime.

"I know with you Greeks the profession of philosophy is considered a kind of piracy," said the king. "I am informed that there is none like yourself, though there are many who, like common robbers, put on the dress of a philosopher and strut about in loose flowing garments which belong to other men. And as pirates, with the sword of justice hanging over them, give way to all manner of excess, so do these self-appointed philosophers indulge in wine and love, and dress in the most effeminate way. The cause is in the laws, which punish adulteration of the current coin with death, and suitably punish the crime of substituting a spurious child; but if the same man imposes on the world a false philosophy, or adulterates it, no law restrains him, and there is no magistrate appointed to take cognizance of it."

Evidently King Phraotes knew more about Greece and about Apollonius in Greece than might be expected of any ordinary man. His description of the candidature for the philosophical life in India is in vast contrast to the state of affairs he speaks of in Greece, yet he had, with a twinkle in his eye called himself a "barbarian." This is what he says:

"With us there are but few who make philosophy their study; and they who do are tried and examined in the following manner. A young man, when he has reached his eighteenth year (which, I suppose with you, is the age of puberty) must go beyond the river Hyphasis, and see those men to whom you are going. When he comes into their presence he must make a public declaration of studying philosophy; and they have it in their power, if they think proper, to refuse admitting him to their society, if he does not come pure. What is meant by his coming pure is 'that there be no blemish on either his father's or mother's side, nor on that of any of his forefathers, even to the third generation; that none of his ancestors be found to have been unjust, or incontinent, or usurers.' And when no stigma or mark of reproach is discovered, the youth's character is then examined into, and inquiry made whether he has a good memory; whether his modesty is natural or assumed; whether he is fond of wine and good living; whether he is given to vain boasting, idle merriment, to passion or evil speaking; and lastly, whether he be obedient to his father, and mother and teachers; and above all, whether he makes a proper use of his beauty. What information concerns his parents and ancestors is collected from living testimony, and registered tablets, which are hung up for public inspection. Whenever an Indian dies, the magistrate appointed by the laws goes to the house of the deceased and writes down an account of his life and actions. If the magistrate so appointed is discovered to have acted with duplicity, or suffered himself to have been imposed on, he is punished and forever after prohibited from holding any office, as one who has falsified the life of a man. Such information as relates to the candidates themselves individually is acquired by a minute investigation of their looks. We know that much of human disposition is learnt from the eyes, and much from examining the eyebrows and cheeks; all which things being well considered, wise men, and such as are deep read in nature, see the temper and disposition of men just as they see objects in a mirror. In this country philosophy is esteemed of such high price, and so honored by the Indians, that it is very necessary to have all examined who approach her. In what manner the teachers are to act, and the pupils be examined, I think has been now sufficiently detailed."

The story of Phraotes himself shows that he had been a pupil of the philosophers. His grandfather was a Raja of the same name, Phraotes. His father being left an orphan at any early age and not used to official life, the kingdom was governed according to law by two of his relatives as regents. They were so despotic that they were murdered by the chiefs of the country, who seized the kingdom. The young king was sent by his friends to the court of another Raja over the river Hyphasis, who had a large and rich kingdom. This Raja would have adopted the exiled king, but Phraotes's father declined the honor. He requested that he might be allowed to study philosophy with the wise men. When the friendly Raja heard this, he attended the wise men in person and highly recommended the fugitive, Phraotes's father, as a pupil. The physiognomic examination proving satisfactory, as they found something remarkable in his looks, he spent seven years with the sages. Then the Raja, his friend, fell sick and sent for him, making him joint heir of the kingdom with his son, besides promising him his daughter in marriage.

This arrangement was short-lived, for the new Raja loved to associate with flatterers, and was addicted to wine and other vanities. So, asking only the Raja's consent to his marriage with his sister, Phraotes's father left him in sole possession of the kingdom and dwelt in one of the seven villages left by the old Raja as a dowry for his daughter, near the dwelling of the sages. Of this marriage Phraotes was born, and his father taught him Greek. There was an object in this since it was regarded as a useful accomplishment for a candidate for the life of philosophy. Phraotes was accepted by the sages as a pupil, a chela, at the early age of twelve years, being brought up by them as a son.

After seven years his parents died, and the sages, though he was only nineteen, sent him to his mother's seven villages to attend to his estate. But they had been taken by his uncle the reigning Raja, and Phraotes had to live as best he could with only four domestics, and a small pittance coming from his mother's freedmen.

One day, while he was reading a Greek play–the *Heraclidae* of Euripides, concerning the restoration of the sons of Hercules to their country–a messenger came from his father's friends to say that if he passed the Hydraotes river without delay, there was hope he might regain the kingdom from the usurpers. Accepting the omen, Phraotes returned to his father's kingdom and found one of the usurpers dead, while the other was besieged in the palace, inactive and helpless. Though, as a pupil of the sages, Phraotes begged for the wretched man's life, he was unsuccessful in saving him.

Apollonius heartily congratulates Phraotes on the omen given by the gods, and later declares in a discussion that the use of wine is antagonistic to any true oracles or visions, for which reason one oracle well known in Greece would not give any information except to those who had abstained at least for the day.

Speaking of Alexander's invasion, Phraotes declared that he had not advanced against the mount of the sages, never having passed the Hyphasis. If he had it would have been useless, for ten thousand Achilleses and thirty thousand Ajaxes could not have helped him to master the place. The sages make no war, but if attacked, drive off the enemy with thunders and tempests, while they themselves remain under the protection of the gods. The Egyptian Hercules and Bacchus once attacked them, but they remained absorbed in meditation until the actual advance on the hill was made, as though they were unaware of the attack and danger. Then, in a moment, fiery whirlwinds and thunders from above fell on the heads of the attacking army and they fled, Hercules even leaving his golden shield behind in the fight. This, on account of its design and its origin, the philosophers kept among their sacred treasures. The shield represented Hercules fixing the boundaries of the earth at Cadiz and forming two pillars of the corresponding mountains to shut out the ocean. These are the Apes' hill in Africa and Gibraltar of today. The symbolism is obvious.

A curious case was to be tried before Phraotes. A man sold a field to another. The latter found in it a pot of gold. The first claimed the gold, as he had sold only the field. The second claimed that he had bought all that was in the field. The Raja would not descend to so cheap a solution as dividing the money, but decided to try the case. He asked what Apollonius would do.

"Without a doubt the man who bought the field ought to have the gold," said Apollonius. "If the seller had deserved it of the gods, he would not have lost the field. If the buyer had not been a good man who deserved well of them they would not have given it to him. Examine their conduct and see if this is not correct."

Next day the men came to plead, and it was found that the seller was neglectful of the sacrifices, while the buyer was devout and a worshiper of the gods. He went away satisfied that the gods had

47

favored him when the case was given in his favor. In this way Apollonius taught his principles.

King Phraotes declared that as Apollonius had arrived in the afternoon, that day did not count, and he was invited to stay until the completion of the third complete day. "If on any account a law should be dispensed with, it should be so in your case," said Phraotes when Apollonius expressed his delight. He insisted on supplying new camels in place of the worn-out Babylonian ones, sending the latter back to Babylon. He provided a guide and a letter of introduction to Iarchas, the eldest of the Sages, requesting him to receive Apollonius as a man not inferior to himself, treating his followers as philosophers and his disciples. In addition, he ordered them gold and precious stones and linen garments. Apollonius declined the gold because Bardanes in Babylon had secretly supplied the guide with sufficient; he accepted the linen; and taking one stone in his hand, remarked, "O rare stone, how fortunate have I been in finding you, not without the favor of the Gods!"–seeing as I suppose some secret virtue in it–ingenuously adds the recorder Philostratus, as if he did not perceive that Apollonius was really referring to Phraotes himself in that symbolical way. A diamond was ever regarded by the Indian philosophers as the symbol of a true philosopher; some of their pupils have been noted for the "art of making diamonds". After all, is not "the philosopher's stone" the human heart made perfect?

Damis and his companions declined the gold, but took plentifully of the precious stones that they might dedicate them to the gods on their return to Greece.

This is the letter of introduction to Iarchas given by Phraotes:

"King Phraotes to Iarches his master, and to the wise men with him, health!"

"Apollonius, a man famed for wisdom, thinks you have more knowledge than himself, and goes to be instructed in it. Send him away learned in all you know, and believe that nothing you teach him will be lost. His power of speaking is above that of mortals, and his memory good. Let him see the throne on which I sat, when your father Iarchas gave me my kingdom. Moreover his followers are deserving of praise on account of their respect for the man. "Farewell and be happy!"

SIX

AMONG THE SAGES

T hree things are said by Apollonius of the Sages: "I have seen the Brachmanes of India dwelling on the earth, and not on the earth; defended without walls; 'possessing nothing, yet having everything.' They sleep on grass spread on the ground; they wear their hair long with white miters or turbans. The only clothing they wear is a short tunic made apparently of asbestos from which an oil is extracted. By virtue of their ring and wand they are able to discover many secrets."

The sages receive Apollonius with hearty greeting and open arms. Iarchas sat on a high throne of black brass adorned with figures of wrought gold; the others sat in seats regularly arranged below the throne, not so high and without the golden figures.

Iarchas immediately asked for the letter that Apollonius had from the King of the Indians, and on the latter expressing surprise at his knowing about it, he declared that inside the letter was a letter D (or *delta*) missing, which was found to be the case when it was opened.

Iarchas remarked that the other men are accustomed to ask a new arrival who he is and what he comes for. "But the first proof we give of our knowledge is that we know all of this beforehand." He then told Apollonius the whole of his family history both on the father's and mother's side, what happened at Aegae, his first interview with Damis, the conversation they had on the way, and what they learnt from others. This was all related by the Indian sage in a clear distinct order, without any hesitation, as if he had traveled with them.

Apollonius was amazed at what he heard and asked how Iarchas came by this knowledge. Iarchas replied: "Thou Apollonius art come to share in this wisdom, but art not yet in full possession of all." Apollonius asked if he might not be made acquainted with this wisdom, and Iarchas heartily acquiesced.

"Have you been able to form any opinion of my natural disposition?"

"Yes, we can discern the different dispositions of the mind by a variety of ways," answered Iarchas. "But noon is approaching and we must prepare for the offerings to the gods, after which we can talk about that. You are invited to assist at our religious worship." Apollonius was delighted with the permission.

The ceremony he witnessed was peculiar. First they anointed themselves with a preparation of amber, after which they bathed. Next they went to a temple, crowned with garlands, and singing hymns with all due solemnity. There they formed themselves into the figure of the ancient chorus, with Iarchas at their head as Coryphaeus. Then with staves uplifted they struck the earth all together, which made it heave and swell like the waves of the sea. By this they were elevated almost two cubits above it. Meanwhile they continued singing a hymn not unlike one of Sophocles's paeans sung at Athens in honor of Aesculapius. The religious exercises took much time, and at the end the sages took their seats, with Apollonius seated on the throne of Phraotes ready to debate with them.

Invited to ask any question of "the men who know all things," Apollonius asked whether they knew themselves? He had an idea that, like the Greeks, they would consider this a difficult question.

Iarchas replied: "We know all things because we know ourselves. Not one of us would have been admitted to the study of philosophy, were we without that previous knowledge."

Admiring the reply, Apollonius next asked what they thought of themselves.

"Gods!" said Iachas.

"Why?" asked the Greek.

"Because *we are good men*," was the answer. So wise did Apollonius consider it that he afterwards used it in his defense before Domitian.

IARCHAS ON REINCARNATION

Apollonius asked Iarchas: "What is your opinion of the Soul?"

"The same," said Iarchas, "as was delivered by Pythagoras to you, and by us to the Egyptians."

"Am I to understand," asked Apollonius, "that as Pythagoras said he was Euphorbus, so you were some Trojan or Greek, or other person before you become possessed of your present body?"

"Troy was destroyed by the Greeks who sailed to its shores, and you are destroyed by the tales told of it," said the Indian. "From an idea that the men who fought at Troy were the only men to be esteemed, you overlook many of a more divine character born in your country, in Egypt, and in India. But since you have asked about my former body, tell me who was the worthiest of those who fought for or against Troy!"

"Achilles, son of Peleus and Thetis," replied Apollonius. "He is celebrated by Homer as the most beautiful and valiant of all the Greeks and his deeds are described as being greater than all others. The Ajaxes and Nereuses are also celebrated for their beauty and courage, but only next after Achilles."

"You may compare my progenitor with him, or rather the body of my progenitor, for such was the light in which Pythagoras considered Euphorbus."

"There was a time," he continued, "when this country was inhabited by the Ethiopians, an Indian nation. Ethiopia did not then exist, for Egypt stretched its boundaries beyond Meroe and the cataracts, taking in not only the sources, but the mouths of the Nile. Whilst the Ethiopians lived in the country now possessed by us, and were obedient to the rule of a sovereign named Ganges, they had all the productions of the earth in plenty, and were secure under the protection of heaven. But when they murdered their King, they were no longer regarded as pure by the rest of the Indians, and the land produced not what was sufficient for their subsistence. Their corn was destroyed before it came into ear; the women suffered from frequent miscarriages; and the land could not support their flocks and cattle. Wherever they fixed on for building a city, the ground give way, and sunk under their feet. The ghost of their King Ganges, haunted them wherever they went, and struck a terror into the lower orders which never ceased till an atonement was made to the earth, of the perpetrators of the murder and the shedders of the King's blood. This Ganges, whose beauty was above that of other men, was ten cubits high, and was the son of the river Ganges. The deluge which was brought on by the father was turned into the Red Sea by the son, in consequence of which the father again became friendly to the land. When the King lived, the earth brought forth its fruits in abundance, but when he died it took ample vengeance.

"Homer says Achilles sailed to Troy for the sake of Helen, and subdued twelve cities by sea and eleven by land; but adds that when she was forced from him by Agamemnon, he became cruel and ungovernable. Let us compare in these circumstances the Grecian hero with this Indian Prince. He was the founder of sixty cities, the most famous in the country. To build will be admitted better than to destroy. Ganges next drove out the Scythians who marched an army over Caucasus and infested the country. To liberate a country is unquestionably greater than to enslave a city, and that for a woman who was, likely enough, not carried away without her consent. Besides, the Prince of the country now reigned over by Phraotes, contrary to all justice, carried off the wife of Ganges; and her virtue was such that he would not break the alliance entered into between them, saying that in spite of the injury to him personally, he would not violate a treaty which he had religiously sworn to observe.

53

"I could enumerate many more actions of this man,", said Iarchas, "were I not afraid of speaking in my own praise, as I was that identical person, which I proved when I was only four years old. Ganges, it is known, buried in the grounds seven adamantine swords, which he did for the purpose of freeing the country ever after of all hostile alarm.* The Gods ordered a sacrifice to be offered on the very spot where the swords were hid, but none could point out the place. Though at the time a child, I took the interpreters of the oracle to the place where I commanded them to dig, and said the swords were deposited."

"Be not surprised," said Iarchas, "at my transformation from Indian to Indian. Here is a youth (and he pointed to one not more than twenty years of age), who is above all men I know best qualified for cultivating philosophy; one who is of good health, of an excellent constitution, capable of enduring any pain of fire or amputation; and yet, in spite of all this, he hates philosophy."

"What kind of disease is he suffering from?" asked Apollonius. "It is extraordinary to think that a man of such qualities, whilst in your society, should neither cultivate nor love philosophy."

"The truth is," said Iarchas, "that he is not of our company, but rather in our keeping: for like a lion taken and confined against his will, he looks upon us with an evil eye, even when we are flattering and caressing him. This youth was Palamedes, who served in the war of Troy, where he had to encounter two most bitter enemies, Ulysses and Homer, one of whom laid an ambush for him, in consequence of which he was stoned to death; and the other deemed him unworthy of a place in his poems. Finding that his wisdom was of no avail and his name unrecorded by Homer (who has noticed many others of less celebrity); and besides that he was outwitted by Ulysses (though innocent), he hates philosophy and deplores his own fate. And this is the Palamedes who wrote without ever having been taught the use of letters."

---

*Ctesias is quoted as saying that the Indians used to bury iron in the ground to avert the consequences of storms and such disturbances. This is evidently an echo of the Indian use of the principle of the lightning–conductor, known amoung many ancient nations.

A FORMER INCARNATION OF APOLLONIUS

While they were talking, a messenger arrived from the King to say he would be with them at noon to discuss some business of his.

"Let him come, since he may go back better than he came, after conversing with the Greek!" said Iarchas in reply to the messenger, as he turned to continue his conversation with Apollonius, asking what his last incarnation was.

"It was ignoble and I remember little of it," declared Apollonius.

"Do you then consider it ignoble to be the pilot of an Egyptian vessel?" asked Iarchas. "I know that is what you were."

"You are right," said Apollonius. "Yet I consider that condition of life not only ignoble but despicable. It is true that a knowledge of maritime affairs is considered as reputable as governing a city or commanding an army; but it has fallen into contempt on account of the character of those who follow it. The action I pride myself most upon in that profession is not one entitling me to much praise."

Iarchas asked what that action was, and led Apollonius to narrate how he had been approached in a temple by a pirate's secret agent tempting him by great promises of wealth and property to betray to them a richly laden ship in his charge. Afraid to refuse for the sake of the ship and the risk of attack, Apollonius appeared to entertain the proposal with every sign of sincerity; and after making all arrangements, sailed his ship as far away from the pirate's hunting–ground as he could.

"Is this what you look upon as a great act of justice?" asked Iarchas.

"Yes, and of humanity too," was the answer. "I think that many virtues are comprised in the character of a pilot who neither destroys the lives of men nor wastes the substance of his employers; and who, above all, conquers his love of money."

Iarchas smiled. "I think you make justice consist in not doing injustice," he said. The Indian philosopher discoursed of the manner in which the Greeks acted upon this principle, even to the point of the poets making the cruel Minos a judge in Hades; while Tantalus, who gave to the men the blessing of immortality is deprived by them of food and drink; and they even describe him as having a stone suspended over his head. Instead of which, Iarchas said he would like to see him placed in a lake of nectar, of which he made so generous a distribution to others. Saying this, he showed Apollonius a statue of Tantalus which stood at their left hand, about four cubits in height, appearing like a Greek some fifty years of age. In one hand was a goblet of pure sparkling liquid which was always filled but never overflowing, enough to quench a man's thirst.

SEVEN

THE RÂJA VISITS IARCHAS

Conversation was interrupted by a noise from the village, caused by the arrival of the king, who came with more than Median pomp and parade. Iarchas declared that had it been Phraotes, everything would have been as still as in the mysteries. Seeing no preparations, Apollonius asked where he was to be received. "Here in this very place," said Iarchas. "We live frugally, for we are content with little, though we have much. But the King will have a separate table richly supplied with all we have, except meat, which is not lawful, since it has life. His table will therefore be supplied with such things as are used in second courses, various vegetables and fruits and the like."

The Râja arrived accompanied by his brother and son, blazing with gold and gems. Apollonius was not allowed to rise to receive him, but the newcomer approached the philosophers like a suppliant approaching an oracle. The Râja's brother and son were treated as though they were mere domestics. The son was a very handsome youth.

After the reception of the Râja he was bidden to take some refreshment. At which, exactly in the manner described by Homer, four tripods approached, as if they were alive, and offered wine, hot water and cold.

Bread and fruits and vegetables came apparently of themselves in the order and prepared as though by the best cooks, and even better. Cupbearers of black bronze advanced, mixed wine and water for the company in goblets made of the richest gems, and acted as though they were living servants. The guests sat down wherever convenient, and no special respect was shown to the Râja.

This Râja was somewhat of a pompous boor, acting without any sign of good manners. He treated Apollonius rudely, sneering at Pharotes and his friend in such a way that Iarchas was obliged to rebuke him, telling him that when he was a youth they made allowances for his extravagant manner, but now he should speak more modestly of philosophy and Phraotes.

Apollonius by the interpreter asked him what advantage he derived from not studying philosophy?

"Only that of possessing every virtue and being one and the same with the sun!" was the conceited reply. Apollonius gently rebuked this vanity.

"Well, what to you think of yourself, you who are so good a philosopher?" asked the Râja.

"I think that I am only good whilst I apply myself to philosophy," said Apollonius.

"You are full of Phraotes!" exclaimed the Râja, sneeringly.

"Then I have not traveled in vain," said Apollonius, as if he could not have received a greater compliment. "And if you ever meet him, you will say he is full of me. He said he would give me a letter of introduction to you; but when he told me you are a good man, I declined to trouble him, when I recollected that no one had written to him in my favor."

The effect of this little trap crowned all the philosophers' studied courtesy and mildness of temper. The Râja unexpectedly pleased, remarked in a low and quiet tone. "Welcome, excellent stranger!"

"Welcome to you also, O King," said Apollonius. "Now only can we say you have arrived!"

"Who brought you here?" asked the Râja.

"These Gods, or these sages," answered Apollonius.

"Do the Greeks say much of me?" asked the Râja again.

"As much as you say of them," replied Apollonius.

"I don't think there is any action of theirs worth speaking of," said the Indian, loftily.

"I will tell them so, and then they can honor you with a crown at the next Olympic games," said Apollonius.

Apollonius turned to Iarchas and said: "Let us leave this unwise man to his folly." They spoke of various things. Iarchas told Apollonius that the King's brother and son were treated so entirely without respect that they might learn not to neglect others, if they came to the throne. The number of sages had no particular significance, as preference among them rested upon wisdom and virtue. The grandfather of Iarchas was elected a member of the college of the sages when they were eighty–seven in number, and he was the youngest of them. He outlived them all, being one hundred and thirty years old. Speaking of the election of the ten who preside at the Olympic games, Iarchas declared that the principle was not sound. First they were chosen by chance, and then, even if that chance should fall on suitable men, they were limited to ten, no more and no less–thereby either including some unsuitable men or omitting some who ought to be chosen. For this reason it would be better to consider virtue rather than number.

Meanwhile the Râja kept on trying to interrupt and asking what they were talking about. Apollonius declared that they were talking of matters very important to the Greeks, but not to him, since he despised the Greeks so much.

"That is true," said the Râja. "But I wish to learn, because I think you are talking of those Greeks who were formerly the slaves of Xerxes."

Apollonius gained an admission from him that slaves and only the lowest of them are runaways, not masters. Then he told how Xerxes had run away from the Greeks in a small boat. If he had fought and fallen he would have been highly honored by the Greeks, but as it was, his memory was despised. Apollonius gave a splendid account of the Greeks.

The King burst into tears on hearing of this wonderful nobility of character of the Greeks. He had met only the Egyptians who had come to India from time to time; and they never lost an opportunity of describing the Greeks as a low mean race, saying that all that was good among them came from the Egyptians. Henceforth he would be careful of the Egyptians, and would favor the Greeks and help them whenever opportunity offered.

The sages lay down on the couches the earth afforded, of grass and soft herbs. At midnight they rose and celebrated the solar ray with hymns, in the same position as they assumed at noon. Then they attended to the King's business, probably some affairs of state at which Damis was not present.

After the morning sacrifices the King gave way to a last indiscretion through going to the opposite extreme of the previous day's rudeness. He pressed Apollonius to visit his court that he might extend his hospitality to him, and send away an object of envy to the other Greeks. Apollonius declined politely, saying he was pleased with his courtesy and thanked him for his kindness, but they were so different one from the other that he hesitated to form any kind of bond with the King; and besides his friends in Greece would be expecting his return. The King was so persistent in his invitation, however, that Iarchas intervened, saying that he treated their holy asylum with disrespect in seeking to withdraw a person from it in spite of himself.

"As he is conversant with the secrets of futurity, he knows any further intercourse with you will not benefit him and perhaps not you," declared Iarchas. When the King heard this he returned to his village, as the rules of the sages did not permit him to remain more than one day with them.

DAMIS IS INITIATED

"Then Iarchas desired a messenger to go and invite Damis to attend, a man esteemed every way fit to be initiated into the arcana of our mysteries; and let the messenger see that proper attention be paid to his friends who remain at the village."

This is about all that Damis says of his own initiation, thereby showing that he had at least learned to maintain silence on private matters. But he tells some of the points of the Indian philosophy, brought out, as is their fashion, by question and answer. As soon as Damis had arrived and the sages had taken their seats as usual, they gave Apollonius permission to ask any question he pleased.

"Of what is the world made?" he asked.

"Of elements."

"What !" said Apollonius, "of four elements?"

"Not four but five," said Iarchas.

"What then is the fifth after earth, air, fire and water?"

"Ether," said the Indian, "from which the Gods are said to have their origin. For whatever things breathe air are mortal, but whatever breathe ether are immortal and divine."

"What element first existed?"

"They all existed together and were coeval; for an animal is not produced by parts," replied Iarchas.

"What!" said Apollonius, "am I to consider the world as an animal?"

"Yes, if you consider it rightly, for it produces all living things."

"Shall we then say it is of the female sex, or of both, female and male together?"

"Both," said Iarchas, "for by an act of self–coalescence it performs the functions of both father and mother in the generation of animals, and is more ardently fond of itself than other animals are of each other, inasmuch as it unites to and coalesces with itself, which coalescing self–union implies no absurdity. And as it is the part of the animal to move itself by hands and feet, and as it possesses a mind capable of exciting it to action, in the same manner we are to suppose the parts of the world, with the assistance of the mind, capable of accommodating themselves to all its different productions. Even the calamities which arise from the sun's excessive heat are all under the influence of the directing soul of the world and never take place except when justice is banished from among men. But this animal is directed not by one hand, but many, which are not to be expressed; and though from its magnitude it cannot be managed by means of a bridle, yet it is easily ruled and made obedient."

To illustrate the system Iarchas takes the figure of a ship, such as the one merchant–ship allowed to the Egyptians in the Indian Sea by King Erythras when he had command of these waters, a law still extant in the time of Iarchas.

"To make the best of the prohibition, the Egyptians built a large ship equal to many ordinary ships, divided into many compartments. Several pilots were on board, all being under the control of a senior navigator of much experience. There were many subordinate officers and hands to work the sails. Part of the crew were armed against pirates."

"Now such is the world under the figure of a ship," said Iarchas. "The chief, and most conspicuous place, is to be assigned to God, the creator of the animal, and the next under him to the Deities who govern in its several parts. And herein we give full assent to what the poets say, when they tell us that there are many gods in heaven, and in the sea, and in the springs, and rivers, and likewise in the earth and under the earth. But that place under the earth, if such a place exists, which is described as dreary and gloomy, let us separate from our idea of the world."

Damis was delighted beyond measure as he listened, and could hardly keep silent. He could not understand how an Indian, even if he had learned it, could speak Greek so fluently and correctly. He remarks upon the cheerful dignified air with which Iarachas uttered doctrines as though under a divine influence, and adds that Apollonius, who spoke with such mildness and modesty, acquired so much the manner of Iarchas, that whenever he spoke sitting (as was his usual custom), he greatly resembled that master of philosophy.

Damis notes that all the sages spoke in Greek, and not only Iarchas, while he was present.

RÂJA VISITS IARCHAS

The sages by no means confined themselves to religious ceremonies and philosophical discussions. As we have seen, they assisted the King in the affairs of his kingdom when he sought their advice, and now Damis was witness of another of their activities on humanitarian lines. For, one after another, people in distress came to the philosophers and were helped by their superior knowledge of nature, men and things, as they performed many actions which the more ignorant of all nations are accustomed to call miracles. Pre-eminently, it seems, their help was sought in nervous and psychic troubles, which the ordinary physicians were unable to deal with satisfactorily, exactly as is the case in the world today.

But physical injuries were also healed, as that case of a valiant lion–hunter with a dislocated hip–bone. A touch from the hand of the sage healed him and he walked upright. A blind man was given his sight. A man with a withered hand was healed. Advice was given in many cases, including the curious suggestion, probably in great part symbolical, that to cure a hereditary desire for wine, in a family where all the children had died from tasting it, the father should search for the eggs of the owl and give them to his next child soft boiled; as a consequence of which he would loathe the fatal liquor which was so disastrous in its consequences to a family thus nervously constituted.

Damis was permitted to be present only at dialectical conferences. The more practical religious sciences and mysteries were reserved for Apollonius alone. These included astrology and divination, futurity and sacrifices, evocations and such things as please the gods. From this course of study Apollonius afterwards wrote four books on astrology, quoted by Meragenes. He also wrote a treatise on the proper conduct of the sacrifices in regard to the rites of each god.

The wise Damis is writing the life of Appolonius and not his own attainments. Therefore we may appreciate his remarks on astrology and divination, remembering that he had passed through some degree of initiation.

"For my part I think the science of astrology and the art of divination are above human capacity, and I am doubtful whether they are possessed by anyone," says the Assyrian disciple. "His treatise on sacrifices I have met with in many temples, cities and houses of the learned. But who can explain with becoming eloquence and truth a work composed by such a man."

According to Damis, Iarchas gave Apollonius seven rings, each bearing the name of one of the seven stars, which he wore alternately according to the particular name of the day. To this time the Arabians continue to call Apollonius *Thelesmatiki,* on account of his knowledge of the talismanic art.

EIGHT

APOLLONIUS–IARCHAS

The discourse between Iarchas and Apollonius sometimes fell upon foreknowledge, a subject which, as the latter was greatly addicted to it, often gave rise to much conversation. Iarchas praised him for it, and said: "They who take pleasure in the art of divination, most excellent Apollonius, become by it divine and useful to mankind. He who possesses within himself the power of foreknowledge, and is capable by it of instructing the ignorant in what can only be acquired by having recourse to the oracle itself, I consider to be most happy, and equal to the Delphic God. You know the art of divination enjoins all who consult the oracle to approach it with pure hearts, otherwise to depart from it.

"For my part, I think that he who wishes to learn the secrets of futurity, should keep himself pure, and free from all mental strain and turpitude whatever. And it is my opinion that a man of this character will utter predictions which he himself and the tripod within his own breast will clearly understand; and that the oracles which he delivers will, on account of the purity of his life, be the more to be relied upon. Hence it is not surprising you, whose soul is filled with such a portion of the divine ether, should possess this kind of knowledge."

They were no dull sophists, these divine philosophers, but had a lively sense of humor, as all true philosophers have, for use in its right place. To relieve the conversation, they asked Damis what knowledge he had of futurity after having been so long a disciple of Apollonius, and there was some quiet fun over his claim that he knew about as much as the old women fortune–tellers who uttered predictions as to stray cattle and the like; enough for himself, though not enough to help others. They all laughed heartily at the quaint manner in which he said this, which need not have prevented him from seeing that there was also a concealed hint in the question that he might learn a good deal from Apollonius if he chose.

DIVINATION AND MEDICINE

Divination is not a science to be despised, though it is utterly misunderstood and degraded in so–called learned circles and universities. Iarchas goes on to show that it is responsible for the whole science of our medicine. Nor does this refer alone to ancient times, for much of our most efficacious modern medicine has been so discovered, as history shows. Divination, declared Iarchas, had rendered great benefit to mankind, of which the greatest was the knowledge of medicine.

"For the learned sons of Aesculapius could never have known their profession so well, had not Aesculapius, who was the son of Apollo, in obedience to his father's sayings and predictions, prepared the medicines most proper for curing each disease. These remedies he showed to his children, and taught his scholars what simples were best to be applied to every species of ulcer, whether new or old. Who will deprive divination of the discovery of the exact proportions of medical potions for every kind of disease and the fittest medicines to be applied in the case of persons poisoned, and the manner of converting poisons themselves into remedies? I do not think that mortals without some knowledge of futurity would have had the courage enough to use the most dangerous poisons in the curing of disease."

MYSTERIES OF NATURE

Discussing the strange mysteries of nature and of science with Iarchas, Apollonius had many erroneous notions of the Greeks corrected, and others deemed fabulous confirmed. Philostratus considers that of such accounts "full credit is not to be given to, nor withheld from them." A wise conclusion, seeing that though many absurdities are held in the popular mind as to the wonders of strange countries, not a few of the most absurd are symbols covering in an unforgettable way most important and far–reaching truths of science.

The fountain of golden water to which such wonderful properties are ascribed is declared by Iarchas to have been unheard of in his country. Possibly he used other symbolism for the same thing. The magnet he possessed, and showed its properties; but the pantarba (mentioned by Roger Bacon in later years) does not appear to be popularly identifiable. It seems to be a combination of the magnet and the diamond, with properties superior to those of both. Described as a small stone, the largest of which is about the size of a man's thumbnail, it is generated in the cavities of the earth about four paces below the surface. It possesses the hidden virtue of causing the ground to swell, and sometimes to open, in the place where it is produced. But search for it is not permitted, because it is acquired only by art, the performance of certain words. By night it gives a light like that of fire of a radiant shining quality, but when seen by day it dazzles the eyes with a thousand glittering rays. This light contains within it 'a subtle spirit of ineffable power,' which attracts whatever is near it, or even at some little distance. If many stones are cast into the sea or any running stream haphazard, this stone or gem, if immersed where they lie, will draw all to itself by the influence of the spirit, and make them form a cluster like a swarm of bees. When Iarchas said this, he showed the stone and demonstrated its powers. It appears to have been either electrical or alchemical, or both.

APOLLONIUS OF TYANA

SYMBOLISM OF GRIFFONS, THE PHOENIX AND SWANS

Griffons are described as actual beasts with membranous wings, slow of flight, but formidable. The account is detailed, but appears to be as symbolical as that of the phoenix, which is just as detailed and yet is all symbolical. The latter visits Egypt every five hundred years and during that time is said to fly all over India. There is never more than one. It emits rays of the color of gold and resembles the eagle in shape and size. It sits on its nest, which it makes for itself with spices, near the fountains of the Nile. What the Egyptians say of its coming into their country, is said also by the Indians, with the addition that while burning itself in its nest, it sings a farewell dirge, as swans are said to do.

The symbolism is very beautiful and ingenious, and the mention of the Swan has the significance that the bird is employed in Indian symbolism to express much the same thing on a larger or smaller scale. Possibly the real old Rosicrucian pelican is the same, and the duck of the Kalevala may be related.

JOURNEYS IN ASIA MINOR, GREECE, AND ITALY

On coming into Ionia, Apollonius visited Ephesus, where the artisans and tradesmen immediately left their work and followed him; some admiring his wisdom, others his beauty; some his way of living, others his singular dress; and many admiring him in every way. Prophesies of the Oracle of Colophon were quoted, announcing him as a man possessing some of Apollo's wisdom, being a man truly wise, and the like. The oracles in the temples of Didyme and Pergamus said the same, and all who needed assistance were commanded by Apollo to go to Apollonius, for such was his will and the decree of the Fates. Ambassadors came from several cities offering him hospitality, since they considered him the best guide of their lives and the fittest person to advise them in erecting altars and statues. These things he attended to by letters and by word of mouth, saying he would visit them. Smyrna sent ambassadors urging his presence, but without giving a reason. He asked them their business, and they replied, "To see you and to be seen by you!"

"I will come," said the Sage, "and may the Muses grant a mutual affection between us!"

His first speech to the Ephesians was from the porch of the temple; not in the argumentative manner of Socrates, but as one having authority. He advised them earnestly to study philosophy and to turn away from their present manner of living in dissipation, occupied with cruel sports, extravagant shows, pantomimes, dances, noise, and debauchery. "Though by these remonstrances he alienated from him the minds of the Ephesians, yet he would not wink at their depravity, which he tore up by the roots, and made odious to the people."

He utilized the love of omens and prodigies in an effective way to illustrate a speech on the community of goods. While he was talking, a flock of sparrows sat silently on a tree near by. Suddenly one sparrow seemed to be telling the rest of something and they all flew away in the same direction. Apollonius noted that many of his audience watched them to see the cause of the prodigy. Without pausing, he went on to tell how there was once a sparrow which saw a boy let fall some corn in a lane. The bird immediately went off to tell its companions, and they all went together to share the banquet. The Ephesian crowd saw the drift of his tale and ran to see if what he had said was really the case. Meanwhile he went on with his speech about community of goods, as he had begun. When the men who had gone to verify the tale had returned, shouting with joy and amazement because they had found it correct, Apollonius proceeded to emphasize the lesson of his talk.

"You see," said he, "what care these sparrows take of each other, and with what satisfaction they divide their goods–a doctrine which is despised by you: for if you see a man who relieves the wants of others, you consider him idle and extravagant; and those who are fed by his bounty as little better than flatterers and parasites. What else, then, have you to do but shut yourselves up at home, like birds to be fattened for the table, and indulge your appetites in darkness till you burst with fat!"

That was the way with Apollonius. His work was to teach, and teach he did—even though the lessons might be unpopular or alienate people of selfish and idle habits. The little homely incidents of daily life were text enough for his discourse.

REBUKES THE EPHESIANS

Soon came the confirmation of his urgency in preaching against the worldly ways and idle dissipation of the Ephesians. They had not liked the rebuke; they liked less the result of their manner of living. For that is precisely what he was trying to demonstrate: that the law of cause and effect is immutable; and the plague was upon them. Apollonius saw it coming, and again and again spoke as though forbidding some monster to enter the land or to pass.

The Ephesians, probably much the same as any 'modern' crowd, treated lightly these exclamations in his discourses, as though they were the effect of fear and superstition. When they saw him visiting the temples and attempting to avert or deprecate the evil, they were confirmed in their careless idea. Apollonius saw that there was no change in their conduct, and thought he was no longer of any use among such a people. Therefore he resumed his travels though Ionia, redressing what was wrong, and always speaking on topics most useful to his hearers.

At Smyrna he took the cup of the city council and made libation of part of the contents, making supplication to the gods that Aegeon, the shaker of the earth, might not destroy the cities of the Ionians. In after days it was supposed that he foresaw the calamity that was going to befall Smyrna, Miletus, Chios, Samos, and many other Ionian cities.

The Smyrniotes took much pride in the magnificence of their city, its wealth and buildings, its art—treasures and natural beauty of landscape. All this Apollonius compared to a statue of Jupiter by Phidias, very beautiful but merely an immovable statue; while a city of good and great men may be compared to Jupiter himself who is not on earth in one place like a statue, but everywhere in the heavens.

Understanding that the people of Smyrna were given to idle disputes, Apollonius declared that a well constituted state should have a 'discordant concord.' The phrase aroused curiosity and discussion which he satisfied by saying that there should not be rivalry but emulation for the common good; not striving for excellence in one thing alone like the militarism of the Lacedemonians, but the variety of effort to make all professions honored and all share in their contribution to the general good of the state. Using a homely simile, he pointed to a ship getting under way in the harbor: as each of the crew did his work in his place to the best of his ability, so the ship prospered.

The plague now raged at Ephesus, and at last the people saw what Apollonius had tried to do. They sent an ambassador to him and he agreed to go to Ephesus, which he did instantly by one of those methods of personal transport he sometimes used. He gathered the Ephesians together and assured them: "Be not dejected, for I will this day put a stop to the disease." Leading the way to the theater he pointed out an old beggar, with a wallet in his hand begging for crusts. This object was in a filthy state and constantly blinked his eyes.

Apollonius called upon the Ephesians to stone him, as being the enemy of the Gods. This amazing order shocked them, especially as the old man was then doing all he could to excite pity and seeking alms. Apollonius demanded instant compliance with his order, and when it was carried out he made them remove the stones. The old man had seemingly turned into a furious maniac immediately he saw they were going to attack him. But under the heap of stones they found no man at all, but a huge mad dog, foaming at the mouth. With the disappearance of this foul monster the plague was stayed, and the city erected a statue on the spot to Hercules, as being the god who had wrought through their deliverer.

NINE

TROY

Traveling to Troy, Apollonius visited the temple of Esculapius at Pergamus, and was much delighted with it. Here he instructed the worshipers of the god how they might obtain favorable dreams, and he cured many of their diseases.

At Troy he visited the tombs of the Achaians and made many sacrifices, but without shedding a drop of blood. Determining to spend the night at the tomb of Achilles, he sent his followers back to the ship and turned off their efforts to dissuade him from communicating with the terrible Achilles, by good–natured banter and wise jestings. He had nothing to do with the Trojans and therefore had no fear of Achilles.

The next morning he sent for one of his followers, giving the name of Antisthenes the Parian, who admitted the name and his descent from Priam. Then Apollonius said Achilles had bidden him not to make the Parian acquainted with his wisdom, because of the blood of Priam in his veins and the praises of Hector that were ever on his lips.

Antisthenes reluctantly departed when he heard this.

The season was autumn, when the sea is not to be trusted. But the people had such faith in the powers of Apollonius over the elements that they flocked into the little vessel in which he embarked. The ship was overloaded and would have been in peril, but Apollonius spied another near the tomb of Ajax, into which he went with his immediate followers.

"Let us embark in that vessel," he said. "It is a glorious thing to be saved, with the multitude."

The shade of Achilles had told him that Palamedes was buried at Methymna, and there he bade the pilot take the ship. The statue was a small one and represented a man much older than Palamedes. But Apollonius found the tomb, and near it he discovered a buried statue of Palamedes, presumably another and more faithful one, for on it was the inscription: "To the divine Palamedes."

Apollonius set up the statue he had found and built around it a little chapel. His praise of Palamedes was unbounded. He called him "this great man from whom comes all knowledge." He did all in his power to appease this great soldier and learned man, who was said to have added the four letters which complete the alphabet of Cadmus during the Trojan war.

In parenthesis we may note that Apollonius had known Palamedes as a youth among the philosophers around Iarchas in India. Those unacquainted with the philosophy of the school of Iarchas will probably ask: "How comes it that the Cappadocian philosopher can talk as though Palamedes were still in the tomb?" Probably the young man who had been Palamedes in a former birth was impeded in his progress by the remnants of the unfulfilled or uncompensated acts and deeds of his former life, and Apollonius in appeasing him in this way might well be freeing the man from such clinging and clogging portions of his former make-up, which really did not belong to the man himself, but only to his earthly forms.

If this is not correct there may be somewhere among the records of the Indian school a tale of the sudden 'conversion' of the splendid youth who had such a distaste for philosophy in his resentment against the Greeks, Ulysses, and Homer. The narrative may be an actual record of what Apollonius did, and at the same time a philosophical lesson for Damis and others, for this method of a doctrine within a history is much used by the school of Iarchas. Rather than a parable of fancy it is a parable of fact.

"O Palamedes, forget your anger you had for the Greeks. Grant them to multiply in numbers and wisdom. Grant this, Palamedes, for from you comes knowledge, and by you the muses and I live!"–Thus pleaded Apollonius at the dedication of his temple.

While passing through the Euboean Sea, the passengers talked, as passengers will. The weather was exceptionally mild for the autumn and they talked of that and of the famous islands as they passed them (as who would not, in that island–studded sea whose dim distances are filled with the deeds of gods and heroes, men and sages); they talked of the build of the ship, for had not Homer said what a dangerous sea it is and to be feared, and might not the weather change before the voyage was done? They talked of the handling of the ship in case it were necessary to avoid the dangers of the land; they spoke of the skill of the sailors, and as lands men do, they talked knowingly in sailor–slang with strange ship–talk and sea–similes. Damis would have none of it. He fretted and fumed and interrupted and finally bade them cease their chatter. The sea was smooth, and the breeze favorable, and there was no excuse of seasickness for his disagreeable manner, as Apollonius pointed out to him, asking what it was he wanted.

"It is because we are wasting time on threadbare themes of no consequence, when there are others of much greater consequence to our hand," said Damis.

"What subject is it, then, that you think best to talk about?" asked his Teacher.

"Subject enough," said Damis, "in conversation with Achilles. You have seen his form and countenance and have doubtless learned much from him that you could tell to us, instead of all this chatter of ship–building and passing islands."

Evidently Damis was learning much since he had been in Babylonia. He was not always so anxious then for the least crumb of philosophical instruction. Now the disciples around were much as he had once been, some were later to drift away in time from even the little interest they now showed, but others doubtless, like Damis, to grow to hunger and thirst after the truth and after philosophy.

"Very well, if you so desire, I will tell you everything; only you must not accuse me later of vanity or ostentation in repeating such matters."

For who of the School of Iarchas will ever tell of such things without a purpose? His first words show that Apollonius had ever in mind the instruction of such as were capable of taking it among his disciples. Does not the word 'disciple' mean 'one who takes knowledge'?

"I obtained the honor of conversing with Achilles," he said, "not after the manner of Ulysses, by digging a trench or evoking his manes with the blood of lambs, but by the use of such prayers as are prescribed by the Indians in their religious ritual for the evocation of heroes."

At first Achilles appeared five cubits in height, but afterwards grew to twelve cubits. He appeared grave, but also affable, not at all full of pride and haughtiness as he is so often described by some of the Greeks. He was of extraordinary beauty. His hair was uncut, as though in honor of his father's vow to devote it to the river Sperchius if he returned safe from the Trojan war.

Achilles complained that the Thessalians were neglecting their offerings to his tomb. He expressed no anger, for he said that if he did, their destruction would be certain. "I advise them not to offer any insult to ceremonies established by law," he said. Even the Trojans, whose perjuries he would never forgive and on account of which he would never let Troy regain its ancient splendor, like other fallen cities, ever cease their offerings to him in public, seeking a reconciliation.

Apollonius agreed to go as an ambassador to the common council of the Thessalians from Achilles as to this matter, because he realized that by so doing he would prevent their destruction. It was his duty in life to regulate the worship of the gods for the benefit of mankind and the purity of the temples, and none could do this work better than he, we must suppose.

Achilles saw that Apollonius would seek information about the true history of the Trojan war, and gave him the privilege of five questions, "such as he wished and the fates allow." In this way Apollonius learnt that Polyxena was not slain by the Greeks on his tomb, but she sacrificed herself in honor and respect of their mutual love, falling on a drawn sword by voluntary action. Also as to Helen, the Greeks were long in ignorance of her whereabouts, sending ambassadors to Troy and fighting battles for her sake. But the truth was that she was in Egypt, where Paris had taken her to the house of Proteus. After the Greeks had found this out, they continued fighting to take Troy and for military honor, regardless of her. Another question was as to the number of great men Greece was able to produce at one time when so many of them fought at Troy. Achilles replied that it was the same with the barbarians, so greatly did the earth then flourish with valiant men.

The final question of Apollonius was as to Palamedes, who was sacrificed to the hatred of Ulysses, and left unsung by Homer out of fear to reproach the character of that crafty son of Laertes. The recollection of Palamedes brought tears to the eyes of Achilles who lamented him as a man distinguished for beauty and valor, though young, as one who excelled most other men in modesty and love of learning.

"Take care of his sepulcher, Apollonius, for you know a necessary bond of amity always subsists among the wise. Restore his statue, which lies prostrate on the ground in Aeolis, over against Methymna In Lesbos."

The cock crowed and Achilles vanished.

TEN

CELEBRATION OF THE MYSTERIES

ATHENS

L anding at the Piraeus, Apollonius found it was the time for
the celebration of the mysteries, when Athens is most
crowded with people from all parts of Greece. There were the usual
crowd of philosophers of all sorts. Some naked in the hot sun, others
studying books which they had in their hands, others declaiming,
others disputing. They were going away from Athens to the Piraeus,
the seaport. All acknowledged Apollonius as he approached and
returned with him amidst many greetings of joy. Ten young men
ran to meet him in a group. With hands outstretched to the sacred
Acropolis where Minerva reigns, to witness the truth of their
assertion, they told him a strange thing.

"We swear by Minerva," said they, "that we were going down
to the Piraeus with the intention of going over to Ionia!"

Apollonius received them with kindness and congratulated
them on their love for philosophy.

Consider. Here were the mysteries of Athens, the religious
magnet that drew all Greece to their celebration, deserted by vast
numbers of those that loved philosophy about to undertake a
journey to Ionia to see and to hear Apollonius, as though a God
greater than the mysteries were among them. These were not the

rabble but the best men in Greece. The rabble were not encouraged to go too deeply into the mysteries, and all barbarians, murderers, magicians, mountebanks, and impious persons were absolutely excluded. Nero himself, the powerful Emperor, was excluded on account of the murder of his mother Agrippina.

These were the people who came flocking to Apollonius, more anxious to meet him than to be initiated–surely no such thing had ever come to pass in Greece within the memory of man or of recorded history. But he gently put them off with a promise to speak to them at a more convenient time, bidding them mind their holy rites, as he himself also wished to be initiated. At other times in history the same has happened, where such a man has submitted to initiation in rites of which he was master and more than master, perhaps for the purpose of lifting up their tone to a more ancient purity. Aesculapius was one in ancient times.

The hierophant was not as the hierophants of old and he had his weak points. Maybe he was even a little nettled that the mysteries were slighted for such a man as this Cappadocian, the Tyanean. He declared that Apollonius was an enchanter, and as such refused to initiate him.

Apollonius showed no unseemly resentment. He answered wisely:

"You say so," he said, "but you do not consider the most severe accusation that could be leveled against me, that I know more of the initiation than yourself. Yet I come to you for initiation as though you were the wiser." This mild but pertinent reply pleased the multitude, and the Hierophant changed his tone, offering to initiate Apollonius, as he "saw that he was wise." This time the Sage himself declined, saying he would choose his own time, when the ceremony should be in other hands. He named the Hierophant who should initiate him, and it actually came about that the one he named succeeded the one who had called Apollonius an enchanter, four years later initiating Apollonius as the latter had prophesied.

At Athens, Apollonius spoke much of sacrifices and emphasized the special nature of the offerings to each god and the time of day when the sacrifices should be made and libations offered, also the hours for prayer to each. In Philostratus's day, 'A.D.' 210, there was still a treatise of Apollonius extant in the sage's native tongue treating of these matters. Such was the gentle and useful way in which he refuted the accusations of the Hierophant that he was not a proper man for initiation into the mysteries. He wrote a text book!

Here also he cured a young man who was possessed without knowing it. His extravagances of conduct and dress gave rise to much talk and popular songs, so that when he laughed with loud stupidity at a saying of the philosopher which seemed at first sight to be fanciful, Apollonius spoke, not to him, but to the demon within, bidding it come out and give a visible sign of its departure. It did this by entering a statue and making it totter and fall. The young man rubbed his eyes as though waking from a dream and stood ashamed before them all, to find himself so much the object of attention and so luxuriously dressed. He adopted the homely simplicity and plain garb of a philosopher and lived "after the rules of Apollonius."

Apollonius rebuked with much severity the degradation of the feasts of Bacchus in Athens. Instead of a manly and divine rite, these celebrations had become effeminate and even voluptuous, in which the divine epics and athletic dances of the warriors were mixed in a degenerated fashion. This is the Bacchus that seems to have descended in a yet more degraded fashion into the literature of eighteenth– and nineteenth–century Europe, not the real divine Bacchus, who is as noble a conception as any in the Greek and Egyptian divine hierarchy.

GLADIATORIAL COMBATS

Another abuse he rebuked was the 'sport' of the gladiatorial combats, in the theater of the Acropolis. The passion for this kind of thing was greater then than it was at Corinth in the time of Philostratus. Burglars, thieves, kidnapers, adulterers, and men guilty of criminal assaults were bought at high prices and forced to fight one another. This was the degenerate side of the passion for public games, which were originally a divine institution. Apollonius was so disgusted when invited to visit the theater that he declared the place impure and polluted with blood. He wrote that he was surprised that the goddess Minerva had not abandoned her citadel, for if the practice were continued to the logical conclusion the hecatombs of oxen slain in the Grand Panathenaean Procession would become hecatombs of men. That he was *declaring natural law*, his power and his vocation, is evident when history is studied. For this is the exact order of precedence that has taken place, notably in modern times in the last two hundred years of the splendid civilization of Mexico before the Spanish conquest.

He bade Bacchus depart to the purer air of Citheron, thereby indicating that the gods cannot or should not live in places made impure and polluted with blood.

From Athens he went in obedience to the wish of Achilles to the Thessalians at Thermopylae. When they heard his message they hastened to re–establish the necessary rites at the tomb of that great warrior. Here he almost surrounded the tomb of Leonidas with a little temple. In a dispute as to the highest ground in Greece, which many thought to be Mount Oeta, visible from there, he declared that where he stood was the highest ground in Greece, because the men who died there in defense of liberty made it so, equal to Mount Oeta and higher than many on Olympus. Ever he kept to the more spiritual side of things, raising the minds of his hearers a step above the material. It was the imagery of the "Above" and the "Below" of the Caucasus.

Visiting all the temples of Greece, the Dodonean, the Pythian oracles, and the temple of Abae, Apollonius discoursed in public and reformed the rites in private, attended by priests and his disciples. He entered the cave of Amphiaraus and Trophonius and ascended the summit of Mount Helicon where was erected the temple of the Muses. The mysteries of the Oracle of Trophonius, son of Apollo, are suggestive of the commencement of Dante's Inferno.

CELEBRATION OF THE MYSTERIES

Once when at the Isthmus they heard the sea roaring outside, he exclaimed: "This neck of land shall or shall not be cut through!" This cryptic saying was remembered seven years later, when Nero attempted to cut the Corinth canal between the Adriatic and the Aegean. Much was done, but failure came at last and the work was then abandoned.

The Emperor showed tremendous energy, but much of it was wasted on low levels. He became a competitor in the public games, the Olympic and Pythian contests. At the Isthmian games he won "victories" over harpers and heralds. At Olympia he was victorious over tragedians.

THE PHILOSOPHER'S ZEAL FOR APOLLONIUS

At this time Demetrius the Cynic philosopher happened to be in Corinth. He felt the same zeal for Apollonius as Antisthenes had done for Socrates, and this he gave as his reason for becoming one of his disciples, and for recommending to his notice the most esteemed of his friends, among whom was Menippus the Lycian, a young man of five–and–twenty years of age, handsome and intelligent, and with an open manly air. This Demetrius showed himself absolutely independent, and even when banished by the Emperor Vespasian, derided the punishment and continued to speak with the utmost frankness. He died a very old man, and Seneca says of him: "Nature brought him forth to show mankind that an exalted genius can live securely without being corrupted by the vice of the surrounding world." Our eulogy shall be grander yet, for he was faithful to the last.

Seneca, too, was among the philosophers, and what he says is of the utmost significance. For is it not these individuals who preserve the world through periods of degeneracy?

Apollonius saved Menippus from the wiles of a soulless woman who had so bewitched him that he was about to marry her. She seemed in every way an accomplished society–woman, but Apollonius declared that she was possessed, and proved it by both demonstration and making her confess that she was a vampire,

81

living on young healthy men. She belonged to a class of the Larvae ("home-woes") and displayed the usual actions when driven away. There appear to have been no lunatic asylums in Corinth at that day, so it was natural to find the city, like others, full of all the various forms of insanity, both apparent and concealed; the apparent cases in modern times are shut away in institutions, giving the impression that there are fewer of them. This case was so well known in Greece that Philostratus feels obliged to record it from Damis's memoranda, though he seems reluctant to discuss such matters.

At Olympia ambassadors from Lacedaemon came to request that Apollonius should visit them. They were so effeminate, their limbs were so smooth, their hair so scented, and their dress so soft, and their faces shaven so clean, that he could find nothing of old Sparta and the rugged old warriors about them. He wrote to the Ephori to make a proclamation to restore the old way of life, to forbid pitch being used at the baths as a depilatory, that the old glory might revive and Lacedaemon look like itself again.

A rough letter to a soft people, but they did as Apollonius told them. He wrote again more concisely than the Laconian manner:

"It is the part of men to err, but of ingenious men to acknowledge it."

Which was high praise from such a man as he.

ELEVEN

ATHENS, CRETE, AND ROME

MEANING BEHIND APPEARANCE

Observing the brazen statue of Milo standing on the discus and holding in the left hand a pomegranate, while the right was outstretched with the fingers very close together, the popular explanation of the attitude is contrasted with the inner significance. The tightly clasped fingers were said to show his strength, the fillet round his head was to indicate his modesty, and the feet close together on the discus showed that he was so strong that he could defy anyone to move him. Apollonius, ever on the alert to teach, acknowledged that the story was ingenious, but that the real meaning was slightly different. The people of Crotona made him a priest of Juno, hence the sacred fillet. From his position on the small buckler it is to be seen that he made his supplications to Juno in that way; the right hand held out indicates the same. The inseparable position of the fingers shows the excellence of ancient sculpture. The pomegranate is sacred to Juno.

A lesson within a lesson and a lesson within that. All that is here publicly stated is little more than a disguised statement that there is a real meaning in such statues, just as in some philosophies there is not an ancient building that does not tell its divine story, its sublime masonry of the divine architects. The pomegranate with its interior full of seeds indicates, in the esotericism of the mysteries, the fecundity of nature, the wife of the Deus Pater, Jupiter. Doubtless the symbolism would be worth following more closely for symbologists, but here the important thing is that Apollonius is indicating that deeper teachings exist, to those who know enough to apprehend his meaning.

He praised the Eleans for their order and decency, which were a passion with them. They were as anxious for public approval as the athletes. Apollonius, asked for his opinion, said: "I know not if they are to be called wise; but they certainly are sophist." That Philostratus wrote this with his tongue in his cheek it is not to be doubted. Why should he not have his little joke as much as any other Roman orator of the the early third century? He was himself of such superior eloquence that the title Sophist was conferred on him. Whether the Empress Julia Domna regarded him as also a wise man, there is nothing to show. But from some of the things he says, it may be that he was not unconnected with a wise school of which she may have been an ornament and Apollonius himself a founder. Such a man does not depart after about a hundred years of intense activity without some of his schools lasting awhile.

A young author full of conceit wished to show Apollonius a bulky poem he had composed in honor of Jupiter. He doubtless wanted Apollonius's opinion, so long as that opinion spelt praise; it hardly occurred to him that he merited anything else. Apollonius was very ironical and led the conversation round in such a way as to show that the young man might very well have written a panegyric of his father, but that he feared he would bring ridicule by his fulsome praises of so excellent a man.

"And yet you dare to praise the Father of Gods and men, without any fear of him or apprehension of being engaged in a work surpassing all human ability," thundered Apollonius in one of his apparent rages.

While at Olympia, Apollonius discoursed on topics useful to mankind, fortitude, wisdom, temperance, and all the virtues.

This was in the porch of the temple. The Lacedemonians ran to him in crowds and in the presence of Jupiter pronounced him their guest, the father and director of the young, and the ornament of the old. These were the men who had taken his apparently harsh letter so seriously and good–naturedly and to them, it appears, came the reward of their action in this attention they received from the greatest man in the world of their day.

A Corinthian was touched to the quick by this enthusiasm and sneered at the Spartans.

"Are you going to honor him with a Theophany, as if a god had actually appeared among you?" he asked in scorn.

"By Castor and Pollux, we are ready for it!" they cried. And they would have done it but Apollonius did not permit, fearing to create envyings and jealousies.

It was indeed the fulfillment of the saying of Iarchas that he would be recognized as a god while he was yet living. Yet this one of the two extremes the gods avoid when they appear among men; either they are called devils and stoned or crucified, or they are worshiped blindly, in either of which cases their mission remains unfulfilled to the public, to make men make themselves better.

Passing Mount Taygetus he entered Lacedaemon and found the magistrates engaged in the zealous observance of the laws of Lycurgus, and the inhabitants all busy about their own affairs. He determined to give the magistrates the benefit of his views if they so desired, seeing that they knew how to profit from them.

He told them the gods were to be worshiped as masters, and the heroes as fathers, but how men were to be honored was not a question that Sparta should ask. Laws are excellent masters and masters will be applauded in proportion to the diligence and industry of their pupils.

Of fortitude, he said: "Use it if you have it!"

The Emperor Claudius wrote to the Lacedemonians about the improper use they made of their liberty of which they were accused by the Proconsul of Greece. The Lacedemonians debated whether to send back a lofty answer or to deprecate the wrath of Caesar. They consulted Apollonius.

His answer was on middle lines. "Palamedes invented letters," he said, "to the end that men might know, not only what to write, but also what not to write." In this way he dissuaded the Lacedemonians from too much audacity and from excessive timidity in their reply.

Apollonius intended visiting Rome, but a vision induced him to go to Crete first. This he did, taking with him his whole company and their domestics.

ROME AND NERO

When he arrived in Rome he found philosophy in much disfavor with the Emperor Nero, who suspected all philosophers of concealing evil magic under that name. One Musonius was such a philosopher, regarded as second to Apollonius. He was in prison, and only a robust constitution saved him from death. In such circumstances it required a vast courage for a philosopher to approach the Imperial city, much more so for one like Apollonius, with a whole school of philosophers in his train.

A hundred and twenty stadia from Rome the party met Philolaus of Citium in Crete, a man of eloquence but not fitted for suffering persecution. He exhorted Apollonius to bow before the storm and not to go to Rome, frequently casting fearful glances behind him while he spoke, as though he might be overheard. Philolaus described the Emperor as driving a chariot by day, singing on the public stage, as living with gladiators and actually as one of their company killing men in combat. Such was the low condition of the most powerful monarch of the time.

Philolaus failed to persuade Apollonius. Damis attempted to counteract his fearful warnings lest the young disciples should be terrified and depart. But Apollonius told him it was a god– given opportunity to test their devotion to philosophy. Some declared they were sick, others that they were unprovided for the journey, business affairs at home claimed some, and unlucky dreams warned others. Thus of the thirty–four disciples, eight alone were found faithful. The rest fled through fear of Nero and philosophy. Among those who remained were Menippus, the one saved from the vampire woman, Dioscorides the Egyptian, and Damis. These three, and the other faithful five, Apollonius called true philosophers, and promised to teach them all that he knew, while refraining from calling the deserters cowards. "But first it is our duty to thank the gods by whose assistance both they and we have been inspired with such sentiment, and next to solicit their direction and guidance on our journey, for without them we are nothing."

Apollonius told in detail the history of Nero and what a tyrant he was, worse than any wild beast; how he had murdered his own mother in an artificial shipwreck, and had committed other fearful excesses. But however terrible he might be, no true philosopher should know fear. "Nothing is terrible to men who have made the maxims of temperance and wisdom the rules of their lives." Bound more closely into mutual companionship by these words, the party went on their way to Rome.

They entered the city unquestioned by the guards, who marveled at their singular dress, strange enough but obviously of a religious significance rather than that of quacks or mountebacks. At a public hostel near the gate they ordered a late meal, and came across one of the strange sights of Rome, in the shape of a drunken musician who was paid a salary to sing the verses of Nero all over the city. He was licensed to arraign all as traitors who did not listen with attention or who refused to pay him. He had a harp and a little box with a precious string which Nero himself had played upon. He sang various extracts from Nero's compositions, his *Orestea* and *Antigone* and other tragedies. Discordant as they were on Nero's lips, this man yet made them more or less pleasing with his variations.

Seeing that Apollonius and his companions paid him little or no attention, he exclaimed that they were the enemies of the divine voice of Nero and had violated the majesty of the Emperor. The philosophers seemed little concerned at this, but Apollonius said it was not their business to show signs of dissatisfaction, and decided to pay him. It was his tribute to Caesar.

In the morning, Apollonius was sent for by one of the consuls who had a leaning towards philosophy and was a religious man. This is that Telesinus who in the reign of Domitian preferred exile from his home rather than give up philosophy.

"Why do you wear that peculiar dress?" he asked.

"Because it is ours and not taken from any living creature."

"What is that wisdom you possess?" asked the consul again.

"It is divine instinct which teaches what prayers and sacrifices are most proper to be made to the gods," replied Apollonius.

"Is there any philosopher who does not know this?"

"Very many," said Apollonius. "But if a philosopher is well informed in these things, it will be much to his advantage to learn from one wiser than himself, that what he knows, he knows well."

At once this singular method of reply convinced Telesinus that he was talking with no less a man than the renowned Apollonius. He forebore to ask his name, in case the latter wished to keep it secret. But his next question was based on knowing his quality.

"What do you pray for when you approach the altars?"

"That justice may prevail; that the laws may not be broken; that wise men may be poor, and the rest of mankind rich, but not by fraud."

"What! Do you think you will obtain such great things by asking?" said Telesinus.

"Yes, I do. For when I approach the altars, I include every request in my one prayer, 'Grant O ye Gods, all that is convenient for me!' If the gods consider me good, I hope to obtain more than I ask, but if they number me with the wicked, I know the contrary of what I ask will be given, and I will not blame the gods for judging me undeserving of their favors through my demerits."

This philosophy astonished Telesinus. He desired to show Apollonius all respect, and said: "Be it lawful for you to enter all the temples. I will write to the priests to receive you and submit to your superior orders."

88

"Would they not receive me without your written commands?" asked Apollonius.

"No," said Telesinus. "The permission depends on my position as Pontifex Maximus."

"I am glad so illustrious a man fills the office," said Apollonius. "At the same time I would have you know that I would prefer to dwell in temples not so vigilantly guarded. None of the gods rejects me, and all give me the protection of their roof. This is all the permission I ask, and it is not denied me even by the barbarians."

"If that is so," replied Telesinus, "the barbarians are beforehand with us in such a praiseworthy attention, and I wish it were said of ourselves."

After this Apollonius dwelt in the temples and he dwelt in none without making some reformations. In this way he passed from temple to temple, and there was some gossip which he settled by declaring that as the gods do not always dwell in the heavens but visit Ethiopia and Olympus by turns, and sometimes Mount Athos, so it was proper for men to visit all the gods. A valuable lesson in toleration.

While he instructed people in the temples they were more than usually crowded with attentive worshipers; also the publicity of his teachings prevented any being misreported. He visited no man, nor ever paid his court to the great and powerful. He received all with civility and what he said to them he said to all the world.

THE ROMAN EMPEROR NERO

THE ROMAN EMPEROR VESPASIAN

TWELVE

ROME

The philosopher Demetrius,–so noted for his independence and outspoken manner, for which he afterwards suffered banishment, although characterized by Seneca as an example of exalted genius uncorrupted in a world of corruption–came to Rome about this time. He was so devoted to Apollonius that suspicion was aroused. Even that devotion was whispered to be the result of selfish magic. Then it was supposed that Apollonius might be behind his acts, of which an example is quoted.

Nero was celebrating the anniversary of the completion of his wonderful gymnasium, the admiration of Rome. The senate and the equestrian order were assembled, and the sacrifices performed with full ceremony. It was a great triumph for Nero. Then Demetrius entered and pronounced an oration stigmatizing all who bathed in it as effeminate; he declared that the expense was an extravagant waste.

Undoubtedly he would have lost his life, but Nero that day was vastly pleased with the world in general for he had outdone himself in singing, not a very difficult matter, one may suppose, for a man with such an unpleasant discordant voice! This he had done in a tavern, a public house–a saloon,–near the gymnasium, naked but for a girdle tied round his waist, which scanty clothing distinguished him from the dramshop habitues, since they had not even a girdle.

SECRET POLICE

Tigellinus, however, who was practically the Chief of Police, banished Demetrius from the city for his daring. This Tigellinus was a type of the average corrupt office–holder. He kept a "vigilant but silent eye" over Apollonius, having every little word and deed however small or innocent reported to him. One fact was held to be very suspicious when a clap of thunder occurred during an eclipse. The great Cappadocian raised his eyes at this unknown prodigy and said: "A great event shall or shall not happen." Not exactly what one might call a committal statement, but when three days later a thunderbolt fell on the table while Nero sat at supper and smashed the cup he was raising to his lips to drink from, it was understood.

Tigellinus did not know what to make of it. He supposed Apollinus must be deeply skilled in divine matters and was afraid, but kept it to himself in silence. He still maintained his spy–system, however, so that he was informed if Apollonius said anything, or if, on the other hand, he said nothing. If the Cappadocian went for a walk, it was immediately reported. If he didn't go for a walk, but stayed at home, that was reported too. If he had his dinner by himself, Tigellinus was kept posted by his sleuths, but if Apollonius had a guest, ah, that was something that had to be reported and entered in his dossier; if Apollonius sacrificed, it had to be told; if he did not sacrifice, then there was something suspicious about it, never a doubt. In fact the secret police of Tigellinus did what secret police have always done when dealing with a man whose life is so absolutely and philosophically straightforward that he differed from the folk around him, from the time of Socrates to the sbirri of the Bastille with their net around the innocent Cagliostro. In short, whether Apollonius did anything or did not do anything, the spies noted it carefully for their chief. Of course, as always happens in such cases, they condemned him on some utterly futile charge.

This time it was an outbreak of asthma or 'flu.' The physician thought they might as well call it a catarrh as call it anything else. But when the raucous divine voice of their prize fighting Nero was affected, then the matter became serious. The temples were crowded with votaries offering prayers for his recovery. That dreadful fellow Apollonius, however, never said a word; he did not even rebuke these hypocritical devotees of their vaudeville Emperor, the ruler of all the world that mattered. Menippus was not so indifferent. He could hardly contain himself with indignation.

"Restrain yourself," said Apollonius. "The gods may be forgiven if they take pleasure in the company of clowns and jesters."

Reported to the chief of police, of course. This time they had caught their man. Immediate arrest on a charge of high treason or *lèse–majesté* followed, and one of the cleverest of the informers or spies or shyster lawyers in the place was ready with his cunningly contrived accusation which the innocence of a baby could not escape. This man was an artist, a specialist, a detective par excellence. Had he not brought ruin to many and many a man, and was he not full of such Olympian triumphs?

What a scene in that Roman police–court! The cards were stacked, the case was forejudged, and yet none could say that it was not a fair trial, since all the forms of law were there, exactly as in the case of the child Joan of Arc centuries later. But Apollonius was not a child and Tigellinus was not Bishop Cauchon.

The lawyer was in high spirits. He flourished his scroll of the accusation before Apollonius as though it were a sword. "This weapon has a sharp edge," he boasted. "Your hour has come at last!"

Tigellinus took the scroll and unfolded it. It was a perfect blank. So were the faces of his accusers!

Tigellinus was impressed, as well he might be. He took Apollonius into the private room of the court where the most solemn business was conducted. He cleared the court and interviewed his prisoner alone.

"Who are you?" he asked.

Apollonius told him his name, and that of his father and his country; also the use he made of philosophy, which was to know gods and men. "But to know oneself," he said, "that is the most difficult of all things!"

"How is it you discover demons, and the apparitions of spec-ters?" asked his interlocutor, who was an impious man and one who encouraged and supported Nero in his cruelty and debauchery and his murders.

"Just as I do homocides and impious men," said Apollonius, not without a suspicion of sarcasm in his tone.

"Will you prophesy for me if I ask you?" went on Tigellinus, quite willing to change the subject.

"How can I! I am not a soothsayer!" said Apollonius.

"But it is reported that you were the one who said that a great event would or would not take place?"

"True enough," said Apollonius, "but that had nothing to do with the art of divination. It is rather that wisdom that Jupiter makes manifest to the wise!"

"How is it," said Tigellinus, "that you have no fear of Nero?" It was certainly a puzzle.

"Because the same Deity that made him formidable, made me bold," said the philosopher.

One more question to catch this wily reasoner in treason, if he could not be tricked into admission of the use of 'magic arts,' "What do you think of the Emperor?"

"Better than you do! You think he ought to sing, and I think he ought to hold his tongue!" was the calm reply.

Tigellinus had no more to say to this wonderful man.

"You can go where you please, only you must give security for your appearance when called upon." It was rather an unusual condescension for Tigellinus.

"Who can go bail for what cannot be bound?" asked his prisoner.

"Well, you can go where you please!" replied Tigellinus. He gave up the contest. His authority could not cope with what he saw was a divine power. It is no use fighting the gods, he concluded, not without reason.

APOLLONIUS OF TYANA

RAISING THE CONSUL'S DAUGHTER

A girl, of consular family, died at the time she was about to be married. The man who was to have married her followed among the mourners, who were many, because of her social position. "All Rome condoled with him."

Apollonius met the funeral procession. He stopped and desired the bearers to set down the bier.

"I will dry up the tears you are shedding for the girl," he said. "What is her name?"

The spectators were touched. Here was this foreign philosopher, a strange man, truly, but one whom many regarded as a god, and who was welcome in every temple, stopping to deliver a funeral ovation, to soothe the feelings of the relatives and mourners, and to enlist the compassion of the passers by.

He did nothing of the sort. He bent over the girl and merely touched her as he spoke a few words in a low tone of voice over her body; none apparently heard just what he said.

The girl sat up and began to speak. The whole party returned to her father's house, as the tale swiftly passed through every gossip in Rome that Apollonius had raised a high official's daughter to life, adding marvels as the tale grew, until it probably became utterly unrecognizable.

The recorder of the history shows his good sense, however, in his comment:

"It is as difficult for me as it was to all who were present, to ascertain whether Apollonius discovered the vital spark, which had escaped the doctors, for it is said it rained at the time, which caused the vapor to rise from her face, or whether he cherished and brought back the soul to life, which was apparently extinct."

It would be well if all historians of great lives were as judicious in their relations. The fact that Philostratus makes such a remark shows that he himself was a student of the philosophy of Apollonius, which was that of Pythagoras, which was that of Iarchas himself and his school.

96

MUSONIUS IN PRISON

The brave attitude of the philosophers in the face of persecution is shown in the correspondence of Apollonius and Musonius, "who excelled most others in philosophy."

During his confinement he deprecated all intercourse with Apollonius lest it might endanger both of them. The letters that passed were taken by Menippus and Damis, who both had access to the prison. Here are several of those that passed.

"Apollonius to Musonius the Philosopher, Greeting.

"I wish to go to you and enjoy your conversation and roof. I wish to be in some way or other useful to you. If you doubt not that Hercules delivered Theseus from the shades, write your pleasure. Vale."

"Apollonius to Musonius the Philosopher.

"Your proposal is worthy of all praise. But the man who is able to clear himself and prove he is guilty of no crime, will deliver himself. Vale."

"Apollonius to Musonius the Philosopher.

"Socrates the Athenian refused being delivered by his friends. He was guilty of no crime cognizable by the court which tried him. Yet he died. Vale."

Who shall doubt that the diamond spirit of these grand philosophers shone in that corrupt age with such a light that it gave comfort to those who suffered for the sake of truth in still darker ages, and yet suffer, with a joyful heart?

The next time Apollonius heard of his unselfish friend was at the Corinth canal which Nero "did or did not cut." He was digging in a convict–gang, but his spirit was unbroken. The fact is a proof that Apollonius was running a very real danger in his visit to Rome and that the eight who followed him needed all their courage. Apollonius was right when he refused to blame the twenty–six who left him on the way.

Now Nero went down into Greece and so great was his fear of magic and of philosophy that he first decreed the banishment of all philosophers from Rome.

Apollonius decided to visit the Western world, said to end at Gibralter and Cadiz. He would see the ebb and flow of the ocean—tides, and the city of Cadiz whose inhabitants possessed a philosophy, it was said, that approached divine wisdom.

All his company went with him, praising not only his determination in making such a journey, but also the object for which it was made.

This appears to have been about the year 66 A.D., when Apollonius was nearing seventy years of age.

THIRTEEN

THE WESTERN WORLD

The great natural phenomenon to be seen in the neighborhood of Gibralter was the action of the tides. That a philosopher such as Apollonius was ignorant of the essentials of science seems incredible, though details and artificial technicalities might well be unknown to him, as being only matters of temporary interest. In the same way physical science would be of little moment to him in comparison with the deeper sciences and aspects of life. It was long thought that the ancients knew nothing of the solar system and the sphericity of the earth, but plain records of the Indian schools are now available showing that all this was known and great accuracy attained. Therefore what Apollonius says of science is not to be casually thrust aside, but if examined may show some useful laws of nature.

He is reported as writing to the Indians that the ebb and flow of the tides is caused by the ocean being moved underneath by winds blowing from many caverns which the earth has formed on every side of it; it puts forth its waters, and draws them in again, as is the case in respiration in regard to the breath. This he says is corroborated by the account he received of the sick at Gades or Cadiz. "For at the time of the flowing of the tide, the breath never leaves the dying man, which would not happen if the tide did not supply the earth with a portion of air sufficient to produce this effect. All phases of the moon during the increase, fullness, and wane are to be observed in the sea. Hence it comes to pass, that the ocean follows the changes of the moon by increasing and decreasing with it."

Reading 'currents' for winds and allowing for the philosophical phraseology, this has its meaning. Apollonius was quite well acquainted with at least some of the actions of various currents, magnetic, bodily, and the rest. He speaks quite plainly of the circulation of the blood, which was rediscovered by Harvey centuries later, but was well known to the ancients and to Apollonius. It is not at all impossible that our own theory of the tides will give place to a more complete explanation when science has advanced a little more.

In a temple Apollonius found characters engraved on gold and silver pillars which none of the Gaditanians could read, none knew what language they were written in, not even the very priests of the temple.

He said: "The Egyptian Hercules will no longer suffer me to be silent. These pillars are the chains which bind together the earth and sea; the inscriptions on them were executed by Hercules in the house of the Parcae, the Fates, to prevent discord arising among the elements, and that friendship being interrupted which they have for one another."

Perhaps this was about as much as he could say without going into the secret temple–story of Atlantis, to which it seems to refer.

IN SPAIN

Comic incidents occurred among the Spaniards at times. There was the royal messenger who came from Rome to order sacrifices to be made in honor of Nero's being thrice a conqueror at the Olympic games. The Spaniard had never heard of the games and celebrated the conquest of a people called the Olympians by Nero. A tragedian coming among them, they were astonished at the antics he played, especially his manner of imitating Nero's style of singing 'exactly.' This seemed to be done by standing on the stage without saying a word. When he began to declaim they were astonished beyond measure at his stage–dress and actions. They fled in terror from the theater!

Apollonius, after much solicitation by the governor of Baetica, agreed to receive him, which he did alone. He seems to have encouraged the governor to support Vindex in his protest against the follies of the Emperor, his crimes and debaucheries. The greatest crime of all, the murder of his own mother Agrippina, was not made much of, as it was said that she deserved all that came to her for bearing such a monster of a son.

ON TO SICILY

From Cadiz the philosophers went to Africa and round to Sicily. Here they heard of the death of Vindex, the flight of Nero, and the invasion of the Empire by Romans and strangers. Apollonius gave a cryptic suggestion that several short reigns would follow, which happened when Galba, Otho, and Vitellius all reigned and passed in a year. The phrase was "Many Thebans," comparing the short reigns of these three to the short reign of the Thebans in the affairs of Greece. The next day he became more explicit when he was told that a prodigy had occurred in the birth of a child in a good family with three heads and three necks on one body. He explained the wonder to mean that none should have the entire sovereignty and some should change their parts as rapidly as an actor on stage. It so happened.

Galba soon perished within the walls of Rome.

Vitellius was lost while dreaming of the supreme power.

Otho within the year ended his career among the western Gauls and had not even the honor of a funeral.

All these things passed within the compass of a single year.

The recorder here takes the opportunity of drawing the inference that those who thought Apollonius was an enchanter must be crazy. He considers enchanters most miserable people who by charms or poisons or sacrifices or 'spirits' claim to be able to change the decrees of fate, many confessing these things. By contrast, Apollonius followed the decrees of destiny and only declared, by the inspiration of the gods, what they would be. And when he saw the automatic phenomena of the tripods and cup–bearers at the feast among the Indians he never attempted to ask how philosophy despises wonderment and attachment in regard to such things.

AESOP AND HIS FABLES

Apollonius has a good word to say for Aesop's fables, as being even superior in their simplicity to the great myths of the poets, which to the profane have a questionable look, especially as the poets strive to make the stories appear true in their dead–letter sense. Aesop, on the contrary, uses absurd little simple tales to teach true wisdom, as man giving a banquet of common fare well served. The philosopher told his disciple Menippus a story of Aesop he had heard from his mother when a boy. How Mercury had given gifts to all his suppliants – philosophy, poetry, music, eloquence, astronomy – forgetting the humble Aesop, who had no great wealth to offer. When he remembered, he recalled a story told by the Hours when they brought him up on Olympus of a talking heifer which had made him fall in love with Apollo's cows. So he gave Aesop the gift of making fables.

This digression is given as a hint to read the fables of Mount Etna with some reserve and discretion.

"I say there are giants, and I say their bodies have been seen wherever their tombs have been opened," declared Apollonius, referring to the giant Enceladus said to be bound in chains under Mount Etna, who is fabled to breathe out fire. "Though I make the assertion, I do not, however, say they fought with the gods, but I assert that they behaved with great irreverence in their temples and shrines. As to all that is said of their scaling the heavens and driving the gods into exile, I think it as foolish to conceive as it is to say. There is a less blasphemous story of Vulcan with his workshop in Etna, but there are other burning mountains in various parts of the earth, yet we are not so thoughtless as to ascribe their eruptions to giants and Vulcans."

Apollonius spoke of the causes of eruptions, but as usual and always, did not fail in his duty of drawing moral inference, that to the pious every land and sea is safe, as is shown by the statues erected to two young men in the Campus Piorum, surrounded by a flow of lava, yet untouched, so that they were able to save their parents by carrying them away on their shoulders. Always consistent, Apollonius never fails to present the higher side of things, even at the risk of ridicule by those who hardly even know such a side exists, or at most that it is a very tiresome application of moral lessons.

IN GREECE

Passing from Sicily to Greece in the autumn, Apollonius left the ship at Leucas. "It is not good for us to sail in her to Achaia," he said. His disciple who knew him left the ship at once without cavil or delay. Others paid no attention to the remark. He then embarked with them in a Leucadian vessel for Lechaeum. But the Sicilian ship went to the bottom.

At Athens he was initiated by the very Hierophant he had indicated four years previously, and here he met Demetrius. The latter told him of the fate of Musonius, who yet preferred digging in the canal as a convict to the role of Nero as a harper.

Apollonius passed the winter in the Greek temple and decided to visit Egypt the following spring. The shipmaster with whom he proposed to sail to Ionia was a dealer in little statues of the gods, and disliked taking passengers, so the philosopher went in another, after utilizing the occasion to point out that such a traffic, merely as a means of making profit, was not commendable.

At Chios they did not land, but transferred into another ship which the herald was proclaiming as about to sail for Rhodes. He said nothing and all followed him in silence.

Asked by Damis what was greater than the Colossus at Rhodes, Apollonius replied: "A man whose whole mind is devoted to philosophy." Sometimes he had seemed too severe in his censure of musicians, but here he met a flute–player who really was a musician and understood it in its higher application to the mind. Apollonius discoursed on the harmony of the actions needed to produce music and encouraged the musician. It was not music he disliked, evidently, but only bad music.

To a young man who boasted of his recently acquired fortune and possessions Apollonius declared that he did not possess his fine house, but that it possessed him. The size of his wealth was nothing in comparison with the quality.

EGYPT AND ALEXANDRIA

At Alexandria the "people loved him without ever having seen him." He was received by the Egyptians as a god and as an old friend, with a procession around him greater than that which a provincial governor would be honored. They met twelve men on their way to execution, condemned for robbery.

Now we know that Apollonius had kept strict silence for five years and except with reason was never prolix. But on this occasion he chattered like a gossip with the officers in charge of the robbers. He told them not to hurry, and then went on with a story about one of the twelve who he said was not really guilty but had made a false confession. "See that he is the last on the list," said Apollonius. "In fact, it would be better to refrain from putting him to death." It was rather a nuisance, this interruption on the part of the aged stranger, and the execution was considerably delayed. After eight of the robbers had been executed by beheading, there was a dramatic turn to the affair.

A horseman rode up to the place of execution with all speed. "Spare Phorion!" he cried. "He is no robber, but confessed through fear of the torture. He is innocent! Those who were put to the rack have declared it in their confession."

Apollonius had no more need to delay the men with his chatter. He had saved the innocent. But what a scene! The Egyptians were ready to receive him with the utmost enthusiasm for his own sake and for his reputation. But here was a marvelous and joyful manifestation of his wisdom, his foreknowledge. The applause was loud and joyous.

When he went up into the temple a beauty shone from his face and the words he uttered on all subjects were divine, being framed in wisdom. This temple is said to be the Serspeum, where in the year 415, "during Lent," the wise Hypatia, the girl–philosopher of Alexandria, also uttered the words of divine wisdom, before the Christians tore her flesh from her body and scraped the bones with oyster–shells. Alexandria passed through many things between the times of Apollonius and the martyrdom of Hypatia, some 348 years, but rarely had the city seen such great events as the arrival of Apollonius and the mission of that fearless, god– taught maid.

Apollonius, as we know, did not approve of the shedding of blood. When the Patriarch of Alexandria asked why he did not sacrifice, he asked a question in reply. "I would rather ask why you do," said he.

"Who is wise enough to reform the established worship of the Egyptians?" queried the Patriarch.

"Every Sage who comes from the Indians," was the answer of Apollonius. "But this day I will burn an ox, and I wish that you may attend and partake of its odor, as I think you would like to do it, if the gods show no displeasure."

Whilst a bull made up of various spices was being consumed in the fire, Apollonius said: "Behold the sacrifice!"

"What sacrifice?" asked the Egyptian. "I see none."

Apollonius pointed out the little model of a bull and in addition gave him much information as to the value of fumigatory sacrifices and their oracles. "Indeed, if you knew the wisdom which is latent in fire. you would be able to discover in the sun at rising many prognostics," he asserted.

VESPASIAN CONSULTS APOLLONIUS

When the great Vespasian was besieging Jerusalem he conceived the idea of becoming Emperor of Rome, as it was said. He sent to ask the advice of Apollonius, who declined to go into a country which its inhabitants had defiled both by what they did and what they had suffered. Vespasian had now decided upon his action, and assuming the imperial power in the countries bordering upon the Province of Egypt, he entered that country as Emperor, but actually to see Apollonius and obtain his approval and advice.

Two philosophers in Alexandria, Dion and Euphrates, who were to exercise a great influence in the mission of Apollonius, or rather against it, were frankly delighted, and welcomed Vespasian, but Apollonius made no demonstration, though he too was pleased.

The sacred order of the priesthood, the civil magistrates, the deputies from the prefectures, and the philosophers and sages, all went out in a grand procession to meet Vespasian. The Emperor made as short a speech as was decent and at once asked for the Tyanean, if he was in those parts.

They replied that he was, and was doing all he could to make people better. Damis, being asked, said he was to be found in the temple.

"Let us go there," said Vespasian; "first that I may offer prayers to the gods and next that I may converse with that excellent man." And he went.

The sacrifices were performed, Vespasian ignored the priests and the prefects and the deputies in his intensity of purpose and turning to Apollonius, said in the voice of a supplicant: "MAKE ME EMPEROR!"

Apollonius answered: "It is done already; for in the prayers I have just offered to heaven to send us a prince upright, generous, wise, venerable in years, and a true father, you are the man I asked from the gods."

Would any other than Apollonius have answered so philosophically and modestly?

Asked his opinion of Nero's government, Apollonius granted that Nero knew how to tune his harp, but that he was given to extremes in other manners. As to advising Vespasian in the government, Apollonius said that he had two very good advisers in Dion and Euphrates.

Vespasian prayed aloud: "O Jupiter, grant me to govern wise men, and wise men to govern me!" Then turning to the Egyptians, he said: "Draw from me as you would from the Nile." The people rejoiced that for a time they were free from oppression.

Vespasian, who was then a man of about sixty, left the temple hand in hand with Apollonius, discussing the affairs of the Empire. Nero was bad, but the affairs of the Empire appeared likely to become even worse under the luxurious and uxorious Vitellius who used more perfume in his bath than Vespasian did water, and who if wounded would have exuded more eau de Cologne, or the Roman equivalent, than blood.

"On you, Apollonius," said Vespasian, "I chiefly found my hopes of success, as I know you are well acquainted with whatever regards the gods, and for that reason I make you my friend and counselor in all those concerns on which depend the affairs of sea and land. For if omens, favorable to my wishes, are given from the gods, I will go on: if they are not propitious to me and the Roman people, I will stop where I am and engage no farther in any enterprise unsanctioned by heaven."

Apollonius, as though inspired, said: "O, Jupiter Capitolinus, who art supreme judge in the present crisis of affairs, act mutually for each other: keep yourself for Vespasian and keep Vespasian for yourself. The temple which was burnt yesterday by impious hands is decreed by the fates to be rebuilt by you."

Here was a statement given to a man who had faith. He asked no sign, and one was given him without hesitation. Vespasian was amazed.

"These things will be explained hereafter. Fear nought from me. Go on with what you have so wisely begun," added Apollonius. The sentences sound almost Oriental, almost in that manner of Iarchas, with which Damis says he sometimes seemed inspired. Suddenly breaking off in the middle of the conversation, Apollonius left the Emperor, saying: "The laws and customs of the Indians permit me to do only that which is by them prescribed." But Vespasian had heard enough to fix him in his purpose and career.

News filtered through after a time that Domitian, the son of Vespasian, who was in arms at Rome against Vitellius, in defense of his father's authority, was besieged in the capitol. In making his escape from the besiegers, the temple was burnt and Apollonius knew this before anyone in Egypt had heard of it, in fact, as he said, the very next day.

At dawn, Apollonius entered the palace and asked what the Emperor was doing. He was told by the officers that he had been for some time employed in writing letters. Apollonius left, saying to Damis: "This man will certainly be Emperor."

Returning later, at sunrise, Apollonius found Dion and Euphrates waiting to hear the result of the previous day's conference. Being admitted to the Emperor's room, he said: "Dion and Euphrates, your old friends, are at the door. They are attached to your interest and not unmindful of the present position of affairs. Call them in, I pray you, for they are both wise."

"To wise men," replied Vespasian, "my doors are always open. But to you Apollonius, my heart likewise."

Vespasian appointed these two his counselors, having learnt from his predecessors, as Apollonius said, how not to govern, just as a celebrated musician used to send his pupils to hear the most wretched performer, that they might learn not to play likewise.

Already the demon of jealousy began to creep into the mind of Euphrates. He could not stand the intoxication of power given him by Apollonius, and envied the Emperor's devotion to that master of philosophy. Is it necessary to go into the form of reasoning such jealousy was bound to take? Euphrates, like the French ministers, was for arguing and taking counsel, and deliberating and consulting and formality and hesitation and all the rest. But here was this Apollonius who certainly recommended him and Dion, but only at the stage of "do this; or how is this to be done?" instead of asking his advice as to what should be done. In a cloud of words he shows his piqued ambition. Among them all there is a sentence worth noting as to the popular opinion of the day of the Jews, but the rest is mostly uninteresting vapor.

"For the Jews, from the beginning, were not only aliens to the Romans, but to all mankind, and lived separate from the rest of the world. They had neither food nor libations, nor prayers nor sacrifices in common with other men , and were greater strangers to us than the people of Babylon or Spain, or the remotest Indians."

Even Dion, invited to speak by Apollonius, approved this and disapproved that and harangued the Emperor with a mass of words and opinions.

Then Apollonius, who was a thousand times their master, whether they knew it or not, calmly set them right, and the Emperor too. In a careful and statesmanlike analysis of the situation Apollonius declares that Vespasian having all the necessary conditions, should go on with his enterprise unhesitatingly and without wavering, leaving aside all sophisms.

"As to myself, it is of little consequence what form of government is established, since I live under that of the gods. Yet I should be sorry to see mankind perish, like a flock of sheep, for want of a wise and faithful shepherd. For as one man, who excels in virtue, modifies the popular state of a republic, so as to make it appear as if governed by a single individual, in the same manner a state under the government of such a man wherein all things are directed to the common good, is what is properly called popular, or that of the people."

Apollonius acknowledges that their sophisms and arguments might well make Vespasian decide to retire into private life, and therefore history need not hesitate to attribute to Apollonius alone the making of that great Emperor, and indirectly, his two sons Titus and Domitian, who were each at the head of a great army and who, if not sure of receiving the empire in their turn would become his bitterest enemies and perhaps fight each other, but who with him as Emperor on a stable throne, would support him.

These words of Apollonius gave immense relief to Vespasian, who declared that he had expressed his own feelings exactly. "I will follow your advice, as I think every word you have uttered is divine," he said. "Tell me then, I pray you, what I ought to do?"

This discourse of Apollonius is so characteristic that it stands alone.

FOURTEEN

ADVICE TO AN EMPEROR

I will follow your advice," said the Emperor Vespasian to
Apollonius, "as I think every word you have uttered is
divine. Tell me then, I entreat you, what a good Prince ought to do?"

"What you ask," said Apollonius, "I cannot teach. For the art
of government, of all human acquisitions, is the most important,
but cannot be taught. However, I will tell you what, if you do it, you
will in my opinion do wisely.

"Look not on that as wealth which is piled up in heaps, for what
is it better than a heap of sand? Nor on that which arises from taxes,
which men pay with tears, for the gold so paid, lacks luster, and is
black. You will make a better use of your riches than any sovereign
did, if you employ them in supplying the necessities of the poor,
and securing the property of the rich.

"Fear the power of doing everything you wish, for under this
apprehension you will use it with more moderation.

"Do not lop away such ears of corn as are tall and most
conspicuous, for herein the maxim of Aristotle is unjust. But
harshness and cruelty of disposition weed out of your mind as you
would tares and darnel out of your corn. Show yourself terrible to
all innovators in the state, yet not so much in the actual infliction
of punishment, as in the preparation for it.

"Acknowledge the law to be the supreme rule of your conduct. For you will be more mild in the making of laws, when you know you are to be subject to them yourself.

"Reverence the gods more than ever, for you have received great things at their hands, and have still much to ask.

"In what concerns the public, act like a prince; and in what relates to yourself, like a private man.

"In what light you ought to consider the love of gambling, of wine and women, I need not speak to you, who from your youth never liked them.

"You have two sons (Titus and Domitian), both according to report of good dispositions; keep them, I pray you, under strict discipline, for their faults will be charged to your account. Use authority and even threats, if necessary, and let them know that the empire is to be considered not as a matter of common right, but as the reward of virtue, and that it is to be their inheritance only by a perseverance in well–doing.

"Pleasures become, as it were, denizens of Rome, are many in number, and should be restrained with great discretion. For it is a hard matter to bring over at once an entire people to a regular mode of living. It is only by degrees a spirit of moderation can be instilled into the mind, and it is to be done sometimes by a public correction, and sometimes by one so private as to conceal the hand which does it.

"Suppress the pride and luxury of the freedmen and slaves under your subjection, and let them understand that their modesty should keep pace with their master's greatness.

"I have but one more observation to make, and that relates to the governors sent out to rule the several provinces of the empire. I do not mean such governors as you will send out yourself, for you will employ only the deserving, but I mean those who are chosen by lot. The men sent out so ought to be suited, as far as can be made consistent with that mode of election, to the several countries over which they are appointed to preside. They who understand Greek should be sent to Greece, and they who understand Latin, to such countries as use that language, I will now tell you why I say this. Whilst I was in Peloponesus the Governor of that province knew nothing of Greek, nor did the people know anything of him. Hence arose innumerable mistakes. For the people in whom he confided suffered him to be corrupted in the distribution of justice, and to be treated more like a slave than a governor.

"I have said now what has occurred to me today. If anything else occurs, we shall resume the conversation at another time. At present discharge your duty to the state to the end that you may not appear more indulgent to those under your authority than what is consistent with that duty."

Vespasian loved Apollonius and took great delight in hearing him talk of what antiquities he saw in his travels, of the Indian King Phraotes, of the rivers and wild beasts found in India, and above all, when he spoke of what was to be the future state of the Roman world, as communicated to him by the gods. Quite evidently Apollonius was preparing the world for the entrance to the dark ages, as a definite plan and life–work.

As soon as the affairs of Egypt were settled, he decided to take his departure, but before doing so expressed a wish that Apollonius should go with him. The Tyanean philosopher declined, as he said he had not seen Egypt as he ought, nor had he conversed with the gymnosophists, the Egyptian ascetics. He added, that he was desirous to compare the learning of the Egyptians with that of the Indians, and to drink of the source of the Nile.

"Will you not remember me?" asked the Emperor when he understood that Apollonius was determined to make the journey into Ethiopia.

"I will," said Apollonius, "if you continue to be a good Prince, and to be mindful of us."

Euphrates lost control of his better feelings altogether when he had heard the advice of Apollonius to Vespasian.

"I agree to everything proposed," he said loftily. "What else can I do when the masters have spoken? But there is one thing that remains to be said. O King, you should approve and countenance that philosophy which is consonant to nature, and shun that which affects to carry on a secret intercourse with celestial beings. For they who entertain such unsound notions of the Gods fill us with nothing but pride and vanity."

This was directly leveled against Apollonius, who had the patience to make no reply, but departed with his companions as soon as Euphrates had ended. Vespasian was annoyed and changed the conversation by giving orders to admit the magistrates and to form the new council. For ever after, the Emperor looked upon Euphrates as a jealous meddler who spoke in favor of democracy, not as he really felt but as he thought would be most in opposition to Apollonius. But he was not dismissed from the councils nor was any mark of displeasure shown.

Dion, on the other hand, he loved, in spite of his agreement with Euphrates. Dion was affable and pleasant–spoken, and his dislike of the disputings and arguments was probably the reason he failed to oppose Euphrates.

After the sacrifices the Emperor offered them presents for them to choose. Apollonius pretended to wish for something and asked what the Emperor was prepared to give him.

"Ten talents now, and all I have, when you come to Rome," said Vespasian.

"Then I will be careful of all you have as if it were already mine," said Apollonius. He would take nothing. "But these men will not despise your gifts," he said, glancing at Dion and Euphrates.

The gentle Dion blushed and said: "Reconcile me to my master Apollonius, for it is the first time in my life I have contradicted him."

"I did that yesterday. Now ask something for yourself," said the Emperor.

"Then give Lasthenes of Apamea in Bithynia his military discharge," said Dion. "He was a fellow–student of philosophy with me before he took a desire for the uniform of a soldier. Now he wishes, I hear, to return to his philosophy."

"Let him be discharged, and because he loves you and philosophy, let him receive the usual long service rewards as though he had served his time," said the Emperor.

Euphrates wrote his request and asked the Emperor to read it in private. But instead, he read it before them all. Directly or indirectly, whether for himself or others, all his requests had money for their object!

Apollonius smiled. "How could you, who have so much to ask from a monarch, speak so much as you did in favor of a republic?" asked the philosopher. Euphrates was tried and found wanting, and as in all such cases, turned savagely against his superior in philosophy. He is even said to have been on the point of throwing a log of wood at Apollonius soon after the Emperor left Alexandria. But Apollonius bore all philosophically and with patience, and Philostratus, following Damis, reports the incident with all charity and with forbearance.

The Emperor often wrote to Apollonius and invited him to visit and confer with him, but without success. Nero had given liberty to Greece, to the surprise of all, and the result was a revival of some of its glory and a harmony such as the country had not known even in its best days. Vespasian with undue severity punished some disturbance with a loss of this liberty. These are the letters that Apollonius wrote on the subject.

"Apollonius to the Emperor Vespasian, health.

"You have enslaved Greece, as report says, by which you imagine you have done more than Xerxes, without calling to mind that you have sunk below Nero, who freely renounced that which he had. Vale."

To the same.

"Nero in sport gave liberty to Greece, of which you in seriousness have deprived them, and reduced them to slavery. Farewell."

In spite of this refusal to meet Vespasian again, Apollonius did not conceal his joy when he heard that in all other respects Vespasian governed his people well, as he considered much was gained by his accession to the empire.

APOLLONIUS OF TYANA

UPPER EGYPT AND ETHIOPIA

Apollonius stayed at Alexandria as long as he thought necessary and then decided to visit Upper Egypt and the Egyptian gymnosophists, ascetics. Menippus by this time was entitled to speak to others, as he had completed his term of silence. He, the faithful, was left behind to watch Euphrates. Dioscorides was left also, as he was not sufficiently robust for the journey; Apollonius advised him not to go.

There were about thirty disciples in all, many having joined the eight faithful ones since the desertion of the others on the way to Rome. To these Apollonius quoted the saying of the Eleans to the athletes who go to compete at the Olympian games: "You who have endured labors fit for men who come to Olympia, and have not been guilty of any mean or illiberal action—go on boldly; but ye who are not so qualified, go where you please." Many of the disciples who understood the saying to apply to them as not being fit to go, remained with Menippus at Alexandria. There were twenty of them. Those that went numbered no more than ten.

After prayers and sacrifices for a good journey they set out towards the Pyramids on camels, with the Nile on their right hand. They went in boats part of the way, to see all that was worthy of notice, and no city, or temple, or sacred spot was passed by unobserved. Everywhere they interchanged knowledge with learned Egyptians, whenever they met together. The boat of Apollonius resembled a sacred galley on a mission such as the annual procession to Delos.

On the frontier between Egypt and Ethiopia Apollonius came to a place where four roads meet. Here were heaps of unstamped wedges of gold, flax, ivory, and aromatic roots, perfumes and spices. To this spot the Egyptian merchants came and left a very fair exchange of Egyptian merchandise for what they took, and this manner of exchange lasted to the day of Philostratus. Apollonius compared the trade as superior to that of the Greeks, who ever seek to make vast profits, justifying them by saying they have to dower a daughter, to set a son up in life, to pay a large debt, to build a house, or merely that it would be a shame not to die richer than one's father.

"How happy would the world be if riches were not held in such estimation! And if equality of rank flourished more than it does? Iron would remain black," he said in happy phrase, "if men lived in harmony and good–will, and the whole earth would appear like one great family."

The sages sat in their boat on the river with open books on their knees, talking of philosophy and one thing and another, when they saw a beautiful youth, hardly yet a man, in a small cheap–looking skiff. He hailed the boat in which Apollonius was and said: "I see you are Sages, and as a lover of wisdom, I ask permission to join your company."

While he was approaching, Apollonius lowered his voice and saying the youth was of good character deserving of what he asked, gave a rapid account of his story and his resistance to temptation, choosing poverty rather than to wrong.

When the young man, whose name was Timasion, entered the boat, Apollonius asked his name and story, which after some hesitation he frankly gave, exactly as the Tyanean had foretold a few minutes before. The disciples shouted with amazement, much to the confusion of the youth, but they told him they were not laughing at him, and that the matter was one of which he knew nothing, so pacifying him. This youth Timasion, who had joined them in the district of Memnon, proved a useful guide.

There was a curious law at Memphis that an involuntary homicide should dwell in the country of the gymnosophists until purified and absolved by them.

Apollonius, seeing a man alone in the desert, asked who he was. Timasion said: "You had better ask me, for he will be ashamed to tell you. He is such an involuntary murderer who has wandered in the desert for seven months and the gymnosophists still withhold their pardon."

"I am afraid you speak to me of men who have not much wisdom to boast of," said Apollonius, "if they refuse expiating him. I fear they know not that Philesius whom he killed was descended from Thammus the Egyptian who formerly ravaged their country."

Timasion was vastly astonished. Apollonius told him how this man was the thirteenth in descent from the enemy of the gymnosophists and that he ought to have been acquitted at once of his involuntary crime, and even had it been voluntary they might well have crowned him.

"Who are you, stranger?" asked Timasion in wonder.

"One whom you will find among the gymnosophists," answered Apollonius, who then told him what steps to take to have the man purified by the rites enjoined by Empedocles and Pythagoras, for he himself at that time might not speak to a man polluted with blood. With due ceremony Apollonius bid him go, cleansed from all crimes, after the rites had been accomplished.

The gymnosophists of Egypt are as much wiser than the Egyptians as the Indians are wiser than themselves. But they were taken in by a mean trick played by Euphrates. This unworthy philosopher sent Thrasybulus the Naucratite to them for the express purpose of misrepresenting Apollonius. They were told the Tyanean was going to visit them in order to degrade their philosophy in glorifying that of India. They were told that he came full of refutations of their tenets, allowing no influence to the sun, nor the heavens, nor the earth, but that he gave them whatever motion, force, and position he wished. This is significant of the fact that the Indians knew other things of the motion of the sun and stars and their positions than were common knowledge at the time.

Sowing his seeds of mischief at Euphrates' bidding, Thrasybulus left.

Now here is a little drama of the workings of the law of there being no accident in nature to one who is devoted to philosophy, which forms so important a tenet of the system of Iarchas. The gymnosophists received Apollonius in a queer haughty sort of way, treating him with some lack of courtesy and indifference. Damis was surprised, and while Apollonius was bidden by them to wait until they were ready to receive him, he asked Timasion if they were really wise and why they acted in this strange fashion towards Apollonius. Timasion said he could not understand it at all, for they were usually courteous enough, as they had been to Thrasybulus not fifty days since. He himself had taken Thrasybulus in his ferry.

"Now, by Minerva, I see it is all his scheming!" exclaimed Damis hotly."Well, that man thought me unworthy yesterday to know who he was," said Timasion. "But if it is no secret, tell me who he is?"

"He is the Tyanean," said Damis.

"Then the secret is out!" exclaimed the youth. And he told Damis how even Thrasybulus in his passage with him down the Nile had told him he was ashamed of his mission to fill the gymnosophists with suspicion against Apollonius.

Timasion went out to the gymnosophists, whom he knew well, and returned to Damis with the information that they would be with Apollonius next day, full of their suspicions. To Apollonius he said nothing.

So they all slept under the Egyptian stars after their frugal evening meal.

FIFTEEN

APOLLONIUS DECLARES HIS PHILOSOPHY

At daybreak, Apollonius paid his adorations to the sun and stood, as was his custom, in meditation. While so doing, the youngest of the gymnosophists, Nilus, ran to him and announced that they were coming. Apollonius mildly remarked that they were doing the right thing, since he had come from the sea to visit them. Then he followed to the portico.

Thespesion, the chief of the gymnosophists, commenced with a long discourse based on what he had heard. The gist of it was that they were far superior in wisdom to the Indians because they needed no magic arts, no display, no authoritative tones, but simple virtue and the conquest of desire and envy, with abstention from that which has life. In fact, it was precisely that upside–down view of the Indian life and philosophy that an enemy would make so plausibly credible. Thespesion was very solemn and serious in what he said.

Apollonius in reply declared his philosophy. Not as that extraordinary product of the dark age, the missionary of the sword of the book, but as a merchant with rare and costly merchandise for sale to others who have precious store of wisdom's treasures to exchange for his own wares. He told how the various sects held out this and that before his youthful gaze, but one that stood apart, of such unspeakable beauty as to have subdued Pythagoras himself, called him.

"As soon as she understood I was not addicted to any particular sect, and was as yet ignorant of her, she addressed me in these words: 'O young man, I am sad, and full of cares; if any man conforms to my rule of life, he must remove from his table all animal food and forget the use of wine. He must not trouble the cup of wisdom which is set in all hearts abstaining from wine. He is to wear no garments made of either hair of wool, his shoes must be made of the bark of trees, and his sleep must be wherever he can get it. If I find him susceptible of love, I have deep pits, into which Nemesis, the minister of wisdom, will plunge him. I am so severe to my own followers that I have bridles made for curbing the tongue.'

'Attend now, and I will tell you the rewards which await him who has made me his choice.'

'He shall possess, without a rival, temperance and justice; he shall be more a terror to tyrants than their slave, and shall be more acceptable to the gods by his humble offerings of little value, than they who shed the blood of bulls. When once he is made pure I will give him a knowledge of hereafter, and so fill his visual ray with light as to make him capable of distinguishing between gods and heroes, and of appreciating duly all shadowy phantasms, whenever they assume the likenesses of mortals.' This is the life I have chosen, O learned Egyptian, and which I have done obedience to sound sense and the precepts of Pythagoras. In doing it, I think I have neither deceived myself nor have been deceived by others."

Such was his description of the Pythagorean rule. He said that the teachings of Plato had been so corrupted in Athens by the admission of other doctrines, that the Athenians were not those who had the knowledge of the soul. He turned his mind to the Egyptians when a youth, but his preceptor pointed the way to the Indians as being the parents of Egyptian wisdom, precisely as the Ethiopians themselves had been Indians in times past.

For some reason the Ethiopians were ashamed of being formerly Indians, and they made the most strenuous efforts to conceal their origin.

"You yourselves were the instructors of Pythagoras in his philosophy, which you recommended, and approved as Indians. But now, ashamed of what caused the earth's displeasure, which forced you to migrate to this country, you had rather pass for any other people than Ethiopians come from India. You have worshipped the gods more after the ritual of the Egyptians than your own," declared Apollonius.

Apollonius spoke so well and reasoned so clearly that the learned Thespesion blushed under his dark and swarthy complexion. Damis was delighted, and so was Nilus, the youngest of the gymnosophists, who leaped with joy and running to Apollonius took his hand and asked him to tell all that had passed in India.

Apollonius said he could refuse nothing to those who love science and were of a docile disposition, but to Thespesion and others who despised everything Indian, he was not willing to communicate any wisdom. Thespesion brought out a convincing argument that surely Apollonius would not come as a sea-merchant and expect to sell his goods without allowing them to be seen and examined?

"Certainly not," was the answer. "But if as the vessel touched the beach one came down to it and abused the cargo, the ship, and the country it came from, and even expected the merchant in the ship to agree with him, I would neither anchor nor tie the ship to the land, but put to sea again."

Nilus said: "This time, I take the cable and ask you to share your cargo with me. I will do more; I go on board as a passenger who knows and acknowledges the excellency of what you have brought home."

Then Thespesian agreed with Apollonius, and the secret came out. "Do you wonder that we felt as you do now when we heard of your attack on us, before you had seen us?" Apollonius was astonished, but when he was told of the schemes of Euphrates and

Thrasybulus he understood, though he said the Indians would never have been so deceived, for they were too wise and knew futurity. He warned them of the danger of their credulity; it would surely make them subject to false accusation in their turn, for such is human nature.

Thespesion little liked the long rebuke Apollonius gave him and tried to pass the matter off lightly, saying they were things of little moment and he would like to make Apollonius and Euphrates friends again.

"That may be so," said Apollonius, "but who is going to restore you to my favor? A man whose character is attacked by lies has some reason to be indignant."

Thespesian made up for his blunder as best he could.

Nilus brought a meal for Apollonius with an air of the utmost respect. "The Sage sends this hospitality to you and to me," he said, "I have invited myself to dine at your table, so you cannot say I come uninvited."

Apollonius saw the application of the remark. "Sit down and eat," he said. "I accept this tender of your person and character with great pleasure, as I am told your attachment to the wisdom of the Indians and Pythagoras is great." "I have a huge appetite," said Nilus.

"For God's sake, eat as much as you please," said Apollonius. "You will give me matter of conversation, and I will be answerable for the rest."

Thus was Nilus pledged to Apollonius as his disciple, but the formality in the way of the necessity of the consent of the gymnosophists, which Apollonius pointed out, was of small moment, because Nilus had gone to them on the report that they were a colony of the Indian School of Iarchas. The father of Nilus had been captain of the one Egyptian ship permitted to visit the coast of India to trade. He had met Indians who told him of the school of Indian philosophy and had brought the report of the Ethiopians being from India and of the Indian school. The gymnosophists gladly enrolled him among themselves, though inveighing against the Indians, so that he had the full intention of going to sea in search of the Hill of the Sages, if he had not met Apollonius. Therefore his life had always been dedicated to the Indians, as he had joined the gymnosophists under a misapprehension.

Apollonius asked for a reward for his acceptance of the new disciple. Nilus promised anything he had to give.

"I ask, in the first place, that whatever choice you make shall be made for yourself alone, and next that you shall not trouble the gymnosophists by giving them counsel that will not serve them." That was all the condition Apollonius made. So they lay on the grass and went to sleep for the night.

The following day a great debate on art and the representation by the Ethiopians of the gods as animals took place. Apollonius was for the Greek art as being the outcome of Imagination rather than the Egyptian Imitation, which was degrading as representing the gods. Thespesion declared they were occult symbols and therefore justified. "There was an old Athenian," he said, to clinch his argument, "a man by the name of Socrates, who was as great a fool as ourselves. He thought a dog, or a goose, or even a plane tree were gods, and swore by them."

"He was not a fool," said Apollonius. "He was a divine and truly wise man. He swore by these things, not as being gods, but lest he should swear by the Gods."

Other debates followed on the customs of the Greeks and on justice, the immortality of the soul and nature. It is interesting to students of old philosophies to note that the Ethiopians treated quite as a matter of course Apollonius's account of his former incarnation as captain of a big ship. The doctrine was evidently not new in Ethiopia, any more than in India or Greece or Judaea or Gaul.

When Apollonius announced his intention to depart for the sources of the Nile the gymnosophists declared that he had an excellent guide in Timasion who knew the country well and needed no purification in visiting such a place, wherein resides a divinity. Nilus they called aside and in private endeavored to dissuade him from going with Apollonius.

APOLLONIUS DECLARES HIS PHILOSOPHY

But he returned to the eleven. These followers of Apollonius saw him laughing to himself, but such was their respect for silence they would not ask him what had happened, if he did not choose to say.

So Apollonius with his twelve disciples sought the country where the Nile has its sources, with the river on their left and the mountains before them.

The cataracts made such a din that Damis actually suggested turning back, but Apollonius pressed forward to the end of his journey. In an Ethiopian village he rid the people of a vampire; this was regarded as a great feat of practical knowledge. The incident is described in the quaint language of the time, making it look like a fairy–tale.

Returning from Ethiopia to Alexandria, Apollonius found Euphrates ever more bitter against him. As he had told Thespesion, he bore no malice towards Euphrates, but the latter could never forgive his tacit rebuke of his love of money. Apollonius left Menippus and Nilus to deal with Euphrates, while he himself showed much attention to the latter disciple, whom they had found amongst the gymnosophists.

THE WISDOM OF TITUS

After Titus, the son of Vespasian had taken Jerusalem, and "filled all places with the dead," the nations round about offered him crowns of which he did not think himself deserving. He said that it was not he that performed such mighty deeds, but that he lent his arm to god in the just exercise of his vengeance.

This answer was approved by Apollonius as being a proof of the wisdom of Titus and of his knowledge in divine and human things, as also of his great moderation in declining to be crowned for having shed blood. He then wrote Titus a letter, to be taken by Damis:

"Apollonius to Titus, Emperor of the Romans, health.

"To you who refuse to be crowned on account of your success in war I give the crown of moderation, seeing you are so well acquainted with the reasons entitling you to that honor. Farewell."

Titus was well pleased with this letter.

"In my own name and that of my father, I hold myself your debtor, and will be mindful of you," he declared. "I have taken Jerusalem, but you have taken me."

When Titus was invested with the imperial dignity, he set out for Rome to take his place as colleague with his father Vespasian. But first thinking of what consequence it might be to him to have even a short conference with Apollonius, he requested him to come to Argos for that purpose. Titus embraced him and said the Emperor, his father, had written to him of all he wished to know.

"At present I have a letter, wherein he says he considers you as his benefactor, and one to whom we are indebted for what we are. I am only thirty years of age, and have arrived at the same honors as my father did at sixty. I am called on to govern, perhaps before I have learnt to obey, and I fear to engage to do what I am not equal to perform."

Apollonius, stroking Titus's neck, which was like that of an athlete, said: "Who could subject a bull with so fine a neck to the yoke?"

Titus replied: "He who reared me from a calf!" referring to his father.

Apollonius was pleased with the ready answer and said: "When a kingdom is directed by the vigor of youth and wisdom of age, what lyre or flute can produce such sweet and harmonious music. The virtues of old age and youth will be united, and the consequence will be that the former will acquire vigor and the latter decorum and order by the union."

"But, O Tyanean, what advice have you to give concerning the best mode of governing an empire?" asked Titus.

"None to you," answered Apollonius. "You are self–instructed, and by the manner in which you show obedience to your father, no doubt can be entertained to your becoming like him. But I will give you my friend Demetrius to attend you whenever you wish and to advise you on what is good to be done. His wisdom consists in liberty of speech, in speaking truth, and an intrepidity arising from a cynical (in Greek, dog–like) spirit."

Titus was troubled at the idea of a cynic as an adviser, but Apollonius told him that all he meant was that Demetrius should be his dog to bark for him against others and against himself if he offended in anything. He would always do this with wisdom, and never without reason.

"Give me this dog–companion, then," said Titus. "He shall have full permission to bite me whenever he finds me acting as I ought not."

"I have a letter of introduction, ready to send to him at Rome where he is now philosophizing," said Apollonius.

"I am glad of it," replied Titus, the new co–emperor. "I wish someone would write to you in my favor and recommend you to accompany me on my journey."

"You may depend upon seeing me, whenever it shall be to the advantage of both," said Apollonius.

When they were alone Titus declared that he wished to ask one of two very intimate personal questions. Receiving permission, he asked whom he should guard against in regard to his life, as he already was under some apprehension, though he would not wish to show fear where none existed.

"Herein you will be but prudent and circumspect," said Apollonius, "and of all men I think it is your duty to be on your guard." Then looking up, he swore by the sun he would have spoken about this even if no question had been asked. For the gods commanded him to declare to Titus that during his father's life, he should guard against his greatest enemies, and after Vespasian's death against his most intimate friends.

"What kind of death shall I die?" asked Titus.

"The same as Ulysses," said Apollonius, "for he is said to have received his death from the sea."

Damis interpreted this to mean that Titus should beware of the sting of the fish trygon, with which it was affirmed Ulysses was wounded.

It is historical that Titus died from eating a 'sea–hare,' a fish from which they say the most deadly poison of sea or land exudes. Nero was in the habit of mixing this liquid in the food of his greatest enemies and Domitian gave it to his brother Titus, not because he thought there would be any difficulty with him as a colleague on the throne, but because he thought he would prefer not to have so mild and benevolent a partner in joint rule with him over the Roman empire.

As they parted in public, they embraced, and Apollonius said aloud:

"Vanquish your enemies in arms and surpass your father in virtues."

Here is the letter:

"Apollonius the philosopher to the dog Demetrius, health.

"I give you to the Emperor Titus that you may instruct him in all royal virtues. Justify what I have said of you; be everything to him, but everything without anger. Farewell."

Thus Apollonius, the greatest philosopher of the West in "the first century," gave the Roman Empire two of its best Emperors, as they themselves acknowledged.

The people of Tarsus of old bore no kindness to Apollonius, on account of his outspoken reproaches against their soft and effeminate manners. However, at this time they loved him as if he had been their founder and greatest support.

Once when Titus was sacrificing in public, the whole people thronged round him with a petition on matters of the greatest importance. He said he would forward it to his father Vespasian and would intercede in their interests.

Then Apollonius came forward and asked what would Titus do if he could prove that some of those present were enemies who had stirred up revolt in Jerusalem and assisted the Jews against him. "If I could prove all this, what do you think they would deserve?"

"Instant death!" said Titus, without a moment's hesitation.

"Then are you not ashamed to show more promptitude in punishing delinquents than in rewarding those who never offended, and assuming to yourself authority to punish whilst you defer that of recompensing until you have seen your father?"

Titus was not displeased with this direct reasoning.

"I grant their petition, as I know my father will not be angry with me for having submitted to truth and to you," he said.

Tarsus was not very far from Tyana, the birthplace of Apollonius, and this incident was doubtless long remembered of the fearless philosopher, "the Tyanean."

After his return from Ethiopia, Apollonius traveled much, but usually made short journeys and visited no new countries. He passed some time in Lower Egypt, visiting the Phoenicians, Cilicians, Ionians, and Acheans, himself always the same, unchanged. He taught wherever he found men ready to receive his teachings.

At this time the towns on the left of the Hellespont were subject to earthquakes. Certain Egyptians and Chaldaeans (read charlatans?) taking advantage of the alarm, went up and down collecting money for sacrifices to Neptune and Tellus, the gods of sea and land. They put the cost at the enormous sum of ten talents, but in their fear towns and individuals paid all they could, for these money–changers said they could do nothing until all the money was in the hands of their bankers.

Apollonius drove them out. Then inquiring into the cause of the anger of Neptune and Tellus he offered the proper expiatory sacrifices at almost no expense, and the earth had rest. Seditions and dissensions at Antioch were likewise interrupted by an earthquake and Apollonius, being present, declared:

"A god hath manifested himself among you for the restoration of peace." He drew the lesson that these dissensions would make their city like the cities of Asia, and ruin them. He seemed to imply that a city, like a man, improves or ruins its body by its conduct.

THE ROMAN EMPEROR TITUS, 41–81 A.D.

THE ROMAN EMPEROR DOMITIAN

SIXTEEN

TRIAL BEFORE DOMITIAN

To put it bluntly, Domitian was a brute. If Apollonius, like a human catalyst, had precipitated all the family good qualities in Vespasian and Titus, all the dregs had manifested in Domitian. His "luxury of delight was derived from the misfortunes of his fellow–creatures and whatever gave them pain." He was physically of a very robust constitution, florid of countenance, with overhanging brows and a manner calculated to inspire terror, sedulously cultivated.

Now Apollonius had never shown fear, but he did not approve rashness. If his duty called him to rebuke oppression he did it; if his duty was not in that direction, he did not go out of the way to make trouble for himself or others. He showed himself absolutely fearless towards Nero, and helped to overthrow him by his attitude.

There was not a man in the Roman Empire who feared Domitian less than Apollonius. It might be said that Apollonius was the only one who did not fear him, for even the brave Demetrius had his apprehensions. Yet the tone of all that Apollonius said or did was not against Domitian as a man so much as against a tyrant, and a system of tyranny. In the larger cycle of life, Apollonius was the 'angel' of the Roman Empire and Domitian the 'evil demon.' The greater had to submit to the less, the Higher to the Lower, to raise it and to conquer.

There were three friends of Apollonius: Nerva, Orfitus, and Rufus. Apollonius was closely connected with them during the reign of Vespasian and that of Titus, publicly corresponding with them on the subject of morality. But though he had, on account of their good characters, attached them to the interests of Vespasian and Titus, he alienated them from Domitian on account of his tyranny and pride, and encouraged them to stand forth in defense of the common liberty.

Naturally these three were accused of being traitors. Nerva was ordered not to leave Tarentum, and Orfitus and Rufus were banished to the islands. All three were thought of as possible Emperors in place of Domitian, for their worthiness, and that made them more dangerous still. Nerva's horoscope indicated to Domitian something of the sort, but an astrologer friendly to the former saved him from being put to death by saying that he had only a short time to live in the course of nature. Which was true, but it did not make the horoscope less true.

Apollonius knew quite well that Nerva was to be Emperor, and when, in spite of all the amazing precautions everyone took to avoid the slightest indiscretion in word or letter in those days, he heard that Orfitus and Rufus were banished, he discoursed publicly on fate and necessity at Smyrna in the grove on the banks of the Meles. He wrote nothing and said nothing that he was not perfectly prepared to answer for, since it was a time when slaves, friends, and wives were all spies, and there was not a house but had its secrets betrayed; one might almost suspect the bricks in the walls of having ears and tongues. In spite of this, no informer ever reported that Apollonius had plainly indicated Nerva as the next emperor, but Euphrates was able to report that he had spoken publicly as if to a statue of the Emperor, saying: "Thou fool, how little thou understandest the decrees of Fate and Necessity [Karma in the technical language of the Indian philosophy]. For he whom they appoint to reign will reign; though he should be put to death by you, he will again come to life to fulfill their laws" [reincarnation]. However, it was understood that the words referred to one of the three.

Domitian took appropriate action. He decided to put all three to death. But even he thought it best to do so under color of reason and justice. So, possibly prompted by the informer, he cited Apollonius to appear before him to give an account of his plotting with them.

The reasoning was plain. In the unthinkable event of Apollonius putting his head in the lion's mouth and appearing, he was to be found guilty and then they could all be executed with a fine show of having had a fair trial and proof of guilt. On the other hand, if that troublesome old fellow fled, which, being a pretty clever man, he would certainly do and so relieve them of his constant reproaches, it would be a clear proof of the guilt of his friends Nerva, Orfitus, and Rufus. The dilemma was perfectly contrived. Really Apollonius was a great trouble, for within the limits of his mission he went all over the Empire creating a spirit of courage to withstand oppression. A dangerous old orator, indeed!

ORDER TO ARREST APOLLONIUS

The proconsul of Asia was instructed to have him arrested. By his power of foresight, Apollonius knew this at once and did not hesitate a moment. He told his friends he was going to make a singular journey, and they had some idea he might at last have come to their view of discretion and be going to emigrate to Russia or Britain or the nebulous regions beyond India where there might be a chance of being free from fear of the terrible tyrant of Rome. He did not say to Damis where he was going, but just packed his bag and went off to Achaia, thence to Corinth, and then to Sicily and Italy. Damis followed– he had learnt that–but his amazement knew no bounds when he found they were going into the very midst of the burning fiery furnace, as a younger man might go on a holiday– jaunt to the games.

At Puteoli, three day's journey from Rome, they found the brave Demetrius, who judged it wise to rusticate there at that time.

Apollonius embraced him and in the most good–humored way in the world chaffed him for his love of ease in such a lovely country residence, comparable to that which made even Ulysses in the company of Calypso forget the blue smoke that rises from the homes of Ithaca in the rose–tinted skies of a Grecian sunset.

Demetrius was too heavy hearted to be otherwise than serious.

"What an injury it would be to philosophy, if a man like this should suffer," he said as he embraced the old friend of God, now over ninety and perhaps nearer ninety–five years of age!

"What danger do you mean?" asked Apollonius, as if it were the last thing in the world to occur to him.

"None but what you are ready for, that I am sure!" said Demetrius.

"For if I do not know you, I do not know myself." Then recollecting that even the stones of the ground seemed to have ears, and the birds of the air to have voices to report the least indiscreet word to the fearsome monster that sat on the Imperial throne at Rome, Demetrius added: "But let us not talk here; let us go where we shall be more private. Let Damis not be excluded, for I look on him, by Hercules as the Iolaus of your labors." Always they compared Apollonius to Hercules.

THE ACCUSATIONS

Times were hard indeed when even Demetrius allowed the thought to flit for an instant across his mind that the faithful Damis might be dangerous! Even then as they sat, in a country home, that had formerly belonged to Cicero, under a sycamore tree (best to talk out of doors in these days!) Demetrius spoke in parable as though of those nature touches which ever appealed to the soul of his hearer.

"The cicadas in the trees have leave to sing in liberty as they please, while we have scarce the right to mutter," he said, as they heard the chirping in the trees above. Demetrius the brave philosopher had been taught to be cautious.

"Even Socrates was only charged by Anytus and Meletus with 'corrupting the youth and introducing new deities.' But we find that our love of wisdom is itself a crime; the greater your knowledge, the worse the offense." He went on to tell how Apollonius was accused of being an accomplice with the three friends in seeking the empire. If his accusers had only stopped at that, there might have been something in the matter. But as ever, they overdo their cause most woefully. They accused him of sacrificing a boy that by an inspection of the viscera the secrets of futurity might become known. If analogy in history be invariable, one might almost guess that his accusers were guilty of this very practice.

But there were other accusations, precisely what one might have expected, for human nature changes little. Apollonius, that terrible old philosopher, fast approaching his century of mortal years, was guilty of–you'd never guess in a hundred tries–dressing unfashionably! After this the fact that he was a vegetarian and a teetotaler were enormities worthy of special accusation, and then "they say, you know, that the people actually worship him!"

But whence the information? Telesinus the philosopher, consul of the days of Nero, told Demetrius. But Telesinus was now far away, having preferred banishment as a philosopher to honors, consular honors, as a man of the world. Apollonius would have liked to meet him "but I would not wish him to run any risk on my account, seeing that he has encountered so much for the sake of philosophy."

Apollonius was not above a joke when undergoing trials such as would have crushed smaller men. In fact, he used the power of humor, the saving grace of jest to lighten the burdens of the world.

"Well, Demetrius, what would you advise me to do or say, to calm my fears?" he asked.

"Do you jest with me," said Demetrius, "for you have no fears, or you would not even speak of your present situation." Then he spoke earnestly and very seriously to Apollonius, as if he really thought he could persuade that old lion to run away from danger when duty to his friends called him into it. It was a moving appeal indeed, full of argument calculated to break a man's purpose. But the very intensity of the appeal sometimes contradicted itself. What was the good of telling Apollonius that it was an unworthy thing for a philosopher to submit out of vanity to a certain ignominious death? "Now if a man dies in giving his life for the liberty of his country, or in avenging his parents, or children, brothers, relatives, or friends, instead of the vanity of maintaining an unpopular cause—."

Apollonius said never a word. But was that a little smile at the corner of his old lips? Was he not going to certain death to save his friends? The argument must be changed.

"Why, the very fact that you have come to Rome within the amazingly short space of ten days since orders were sent to arrest you, is suspicious, as confirming your knowledge of the future, and they will only use it as one more proof that you did sacrifice the boy to prophesy by his liver. You cannot say I was not brave in the terrible days of Nero when I withstood him to the face at the baths, and came off with my life only because he had sung extra well that day and was pleased with himself. But I am wise, too, and I say that these times are far more terrible. Nero was a monster, but his cruelties were at least qualified by music, such as it was. This man, on the contrary, hasn't a single redeeming feature. Why, only the other day he killed some musicians because they disputed which had won the prize in a contest by voice and instrument.

"Look at the harbor there and see the ships! Some are bound for Libya, Egypt, Phoenicia, others for Cyprus and Sardinia, and yet others for more distant lands. If you are wise, Apollonius, go down there and get on board a ship, and go anywhere you please, but not to Rome!"

Damis opened his Assyrian eyes wide on hearing this. He hadn't known till that moment where they were going–all he knew was that he was with his master, his beloved Teacher. He was completely overcome at the revelation. There is something pathetic and yet comic in the way he speaks.

"I hope your advice will be of use," he said. "As for me, I can do nothing with Apollonius when I try to dissuade him from running on to drawn swords or into the cruelest tyranny ever known. If I had not seen you I should not have known where we were going! Yet here am I traveling the seas of Sicily and the Tyrrhenian bays and I literally have to say I don't know, when I am asked where I am going. I appear ridiculous. If I had only been told we were off for Rome, I could at least have told people that Apollonius had fallen in love with death and that I was his rival!"

Already Damis sees the executioner before them. "I will say it while I have the chance, that if I die, philosophy may not suffer much by it. I am but the attendant of a courageous philosopher whose sole merit consists in following his master. But if they put Apollonius to death, it will be a trophy for the destruction of philosophy, for he of all men is best able to support her. We have many Anytuses and Meletuses to contend with (he is thinking of the informers who accused Socrates—how could Socrates die and Apollonius be saved in circumstances a hundred times worse?). The friends of Apollonius are accused on all sides, one for having smiled when he glanced at tyranny, another for having justified what was said; one for having started the subject, and another for having departed pleased with what was said. For myself I think a man should lay down his life for philosophy as he would for his altars and his city and his sepulchers, and many are the illustrious men who have died in the defense of such things. But for the sake of destroying philosophy, I would neither wish to die myself nor anyone who loves her and Apollonius."

A pretty strong argument to convince even an Apollonius. But he was unruffled. Yet the situation was serious and his advisers honest, so he took the trouble to go at length into the position from the standpoint of a philosopher, after chiding Demetrius for frightening Damis, who was an Assyrian accustomed to rulers of absolute power, instead of calming his fears. "Neither fire nor sword would terrify a wise man or make him flinch, or have recourse to falsehood or equivocation to save his life, for what he knows he will as religiously preserve as if the hidden mysteries of Ceres were confided to him. My knowledge is greater than that of other men, because I know all things. What I know, I know in part for the use of the wise and good, in part for myself and the gods; but I know nothing for tyrants, let them use whatever threats and tortures they please."

Then he gives them a crumb of comfort, a prophecy of the future exactly opposite to all seeming probability.

"I am not come on a fool's errand. I am under no apprehension on account of my own life, for the tyrant's power is unable to destroy me, even though I wished it myself."

Then from point to point he goes on to show that he could not act otherwise than in the interests of his friends, and that if he did, he himself and philosophy would suffer reproach and he would not be able to face good men any more, least of all Iarchas, and Bardanes, Phraotes, and Thespesion, after violating the privilege of the cup of Tantalus, which required from all who drank of it a participation in the dangers of their friends. "But I will never be false to myself, and I will combat against the tyrant," he said.

Demetrius and Damis both took heart, and the former was actually bold enough to invite them to his dwelling. Apollonius declined, saying that it would be dangerous, even considered high treason, to be seen supping with the Emperor's enemy, nor must he accompany him to the port, for the same reason. But "when times shall mend, we shall sup together!" was his promise.

It was not easy to upset Demetrius but the farewell affected him to an unusual extent, though he tried to hide it, by turning his face aside.

Then came the test for Damis. Besides, it was an excuse to pretend not to see the tears of the brave old Demetrius.

"If you are as full of courage as I am," said Apollonius to Damis, "let us embark together tonight. If not, now is the time to decide about remaining where you are. You can stay with Demetrius who is our common friend."

The long and intimate talk of Apollonius had not missed its mark.

"How could I think of leaving you after what we have just heard of the duty of a friend in danger?" he asked. "What would the world think of me?" But what he meant was, "what should I think of myself?"

Apollonius approved. But he loved Damis and was unwilling to have him run into danger without necessity.

"I will appear as I am; but for you," he said to Damis, "I recommend an ordinary dress instead of what you have on. You should cut your hair and put on a linen dress and go without shoes. I know we must suffer for our course of life, but I am against your sharing all the dangers and being cast into prison, which will certainly be the case if you are betrayed by your habit. I want you to follow me and be present at all that passes, as one who in other respects loves me without being pledged to my philosophy."

So Damis laid aside his Pythagorean garb not with fear or sorrow, but because his master wished it.

Going by sea from Puteoli to the Tiber they arrived on the third day.

The imperial sword was then in the hands of Aelian, the Pretorian Prefect. This man formerly loved Apollonius and used to talk to him when in Egypt, but he said never a word about this to Domitian, seeing that it could only endanger his power of helping Apollonius. Instead, he made light of "the prattle of these sophists, who only do it for advertisement and when they can no longer make a living that way, they want to die so as to depart in a blaze of glory. That is why Nero refused to put him to death, but obliged him to live as a punishment by not giving him the celebrity he sought." Aelian laughed while he talked in this way as if he did not care about it at all except as something of a joke; but he thought to save his friend from death by it. "Look at Musonius the Tyrrhenian," he said. "He deified Nero and was shut up in the island of Gyara (after being set to digging in the abortive Corinth canal). The Greeks made a regular resort of the island, for they love sophists of this kind.

140

They used to sail to the place to talk to him, but now they go to see the fountain there. For when Musonius went there the island had no water; but he discovered this spring, and it is now no less celebrated in the songs of the Greeks than the fountain of the Muses on Mount Helicon which they call Caballinus."

In this way Aelian tried to lighten the seriousness of the situation for Apollonius. But when the latter was brought before him he went further. The accuser, Euphrates, attacked the prisoner furiously as an enchanter, and an exceptional one.

"Keep your charges for the Emperor's tribunal!" commanded Aelian.

But Apollonius asked: "If I am an enchanter, how can I be brought to trial? If I am brought to trial how can I be considered an enchanter? The only explanation of such a possibility is that calumny has acquired power superior to that of enchantment."

This nettled the accuser, as the dilemma was perfect. He was about to bring forward some more absurd charge, when Aelian said: "I want the time before the trial to examine him privately in the silent room of the court, and let none listen, for the cause is one of great moment. By so doing it will shorten the process, especially if he pleads guilty. If not, then it is for the Emperor to decide."

When alone, Aelian told Apollonius frankly the whole situation. How that he was friendly, but that if the least sign of it leaked out, it would be a hard matter to guess which of them would be killed first. "The Emperor wants to condemn you," he said, "but seems afraid to do so without some solid ground of accusation; besides, he wants to use you as a means of destroying some men of consular authority.

"I was very young when Vespasian, the Emperor's father, went to Egypt to sacrifice to the gods and to consult you on his affairs. Being an experienced military man, I went with him as tribune. I remember you received me with much attention, and when the Emperor was away you took me aside and told me who I was, what my name is, and also my father's name. Then you told me I should one day be what I am, holding an office thought by most people to be superior to every human dignity, troublesome though I think it."

Apollonius said: "As you have opened your mind to me, I will open mine to you. You speak like one of my old disciples, like a philosopher, and as you seem from affection prepared to share my dangers I will declare my whole heart to you."

Then he told how he might easily have escaped to a country of the philosophers where no injustice was possible and therefore no courts were needed, since the people were much more pious than those of Rome. But fearing to be a traitor to his friends and fearing that they might suffer, he had come to plead his cause. Then he asked what the accusation was, against which he would have to defend himself.

Aelian told him. His manner of dress, his way of living, the adoration paid him, and the answer he gave the Ephesians about the plague, all were to be brought against him. Then there was every shred of talk that might be twisted against the Emperor, though more of it was done purposely and boldly enough–all was said to have been uttered under the inspiration of the gods. But the titbit was the story of the sacrifice of the Arcadian boy by the light of the waning moon in a field, in the presence of Nerva, in order to bring about the death of Domitian–as pretty a piece of magic and criminal superstition as the mind of an evil magician could conceive.

Aelian begged him not to show disrespect to the Emperor.

"It is to show my respect for him that I come here voluntarily to be tried," he said. "But even if I wished to be disrespectful, I would forego that plan for your sake. I don't care what an enemy thinks of me, but I value the opinion of a friend." In such a manner Apollonius answered the Prefect.

Aelian then delivered him to the turnkeys, assuming an air of great wrath against Apollonius in order to disguise his real feelings.

A tribune meeting Apollonius mocked him while pretending to be seriously anxious to help him. But he failed to score his point, for was not Apollonius so deeply immersed in telling Damis all about the Nile Delta that he did not notice what the tribune said? That was ever the way of Apollonius.

Aelian then ordered Apollonius to be transferred to the place of the unbound prisoners, and Damis was so struck by the coincidence of finding a friend in Aelian that he declared it looked as if a god had tried to lend a helping hand in their dangerous situation. Apollonius rebuked him for his fears. Damis brought forward one or two very good reasons why he should fear Domitian, whom nobody could influence, least of all themselves.

"Do you not see that Domitian is inflated with pride and is evidently insane?" asked Apollonius.

"It is impossible not to see it," said Damis.

"Then the more you are acquainted with the tyrant the more you ought to despise him and all he can do," said Apollonius.

The answer, seemingly somewhat cryptic, is important, for Apollonius was a master in the domain of psychology and evidently knew how to deal with a maniac.

SEVENTEEN

APPROACHING CONFRONTATION

Apollonius was never off duty. No sooner was he among the other unbound prisoners, and there were about fifty of them in a wretched state of mind, than he began to rouse them up and encourage them and show them the bright side of things. Many of them were under the most trivial accusations and suspicions and yet they seemed sure of death at the hand of the homicidal maniac on the throne. To him a house, a city, a country bounded by rivers, an ocean–bound continent, the whole world, were prisons, the body itself was a prison full of suffering. As for the prison at Rome, he had voluntarily come thither, so why should they fear more than he?

The result of his speech to all and every one, was that many who through fear had been going without their meals now left the steward with empty shelves, and smiles took the place of tears and groans.

"How can any harm befall us while Apollonius is with us?" they said.

Speaking to individuals in the prison, Apollonius had as usual been very frank in what he said of the Emperor, just as he was equally frank in blaming a crime or inculcating fortitude. One crime he mentions is interesting. Among other things he tells an accused man that if he has really committed a crime such as acquiring wealth by robbery, or selling poisonous drugs, *or by ransacking the tombs of ancient kings*, stored with gold and precious treasure, he ought to be capitally punished. This to a man whose inherited riches had excited envy.

One was actually under the grave accusation of liking to live alone on a little island in peace. How could a man do that, the informers argued, unless he had committed some crime to make him shun the mainland?

Next day, the same thing happened, and Apollonius began to talk. Even in the prison there seemed to be informers, for a new prisoner came in talking as volubly as an informer when he is making eight or ten false accusations. He said he was in great danger, and did everything to get others to talk, especially Apollonius. But the wise old philosopher saw through the trick and realized that this was simply a spy sent to catch him in treasonable utterances against the Emperor.

How he talked, that old Tyanean! How the prisoners were delighted with what he said and how eagerly they listened to his fascinating discourse! The Emperor?–Not a word! He was talking of rivers and mountains and animals and trees and all the wonderful things of nature. Quite likely he talked, as all those philosophers do, of vast cyclopean ruins, of giants, of flying dragons and pterodactyls that once inhabited the earth, of lost continents and huge cataclysms, and a thousand and one things they had barely heard mentioned in books. Only, as this wonderful old man spoke, you could almost see the things he described. There was no vague speculation, but such a vivid imagery of description as a man having the object before his eyes could not excel.

The new prisoner could not make head or tail of it. He was here to catch the old man. Perhaps the steward had thought he might save more on the victuals if he said that the old man was in some mysterious way putting heart of courage into all the prisoners; by talking against the Emperor, doubtless. Well, if he would not talk against the Emperor he must be made to do so. The informer put it to him pointblank.

"*You* can say what you like against him," was the surprising answer. "I shall not turn informer! And as for myself, I will tell the Emperor in person whatever I think reprehensible in his conduct."

The spy was beaten. How had the old man read his thoughts?

Aelian was evidently on tenterhooks as to what Apollonius would say to the Emperor. At the very least he was sure to insult him to his face, for the Tyanean feared nobody, least of all the worldly great. He had promised out of consideration for Aelian not to be disrespectful, but that might only be the old man's polite way of putting it. So when another mysterious stranger came in and asked for the Tyanean, Apollonius was watchful. When the man took him aside and said significantly: "The Emperor will speak with you tomorrow," his sense of sincerity told him that the message was from Aelian. The visitor asked if he had all he needed, as orders had been given to the keeper of the prison to supply all he wished.

"That is right," said Apollonius, "but I need nothing. I live here just as I do everywhere else, and I talk on the common things of life as usual. I have no wants." Apollonius seemed very amenable to reason and good–tempered, so out came the real message.

"Would you not like the advice of a friend to tell you the right way to address the Emperor?" he asked. If only the old man could be got to let some lawyer tell him the way to talk, there might be a chance of his coming alive out of the Emperor's hands. If not, there was no telling what he would say or would not say, and then the fat would be in the fire with a vengeance. Now if he would only cultivate a little delicate flattery, say,–"

"I should indeed like such a friend to advise me," said Apollonius, "if he could only keep from advising me to flatter him!"

The messenger tried again.–"But suppose he advised you not to be disrespectful and to avoid any kind of insolence?"

"Thank you for the advice. It is good, and it is just what I shall follow," said Apollonius.–Was that a little smile at the corner of the old man's lips?

146

APPROACHING CONFRONTATION

"Well, that is what I came for, to advise you so, and I am delighted to hear you will control yourself (!) and act in obedience to it. I thought it right to prepare you to meet the terrible countenance and voice of the Emperor without faltering. For even when he tries to speak gently his voice is harsh, and his eyebrows hang heavy over his eyes, while his cheeks are so bloated with bile that there is not another man in the Empire like him to look upon. Try not to let these things intimidate you, O Tyanean, for they are really only natural defects."

Apollonius encouraged him to have no fear by quoting the way in which Ulysses faced the unseeing Polyphemus and then returned alive. He would have similar courage. He told Damis all that had passed and said he wanted no more than to escape with his friends for whom he had placed himself in such peril. Then he went to sleep, or seemed to do so. But in the morning he said he had passed a sleepless night and needed rest.

Would Damis ever really understand his old Teacher? Here he had been with him for more years than go to make up many a lifetime of activity and he thought at once the Tyanean had been worrying with anxiety and perhaps fear.

"Yes, you see, I have been thinking all night over what Phraotes said to me," said the old man. Perhaps there was a touch of humor in his tone.

Really he must be showing signs of his great age! "I think if you had to stay awake you might at least have been preparing for the interview; it's not a light matter, that!" said Damis. Had *he* passed sleepless hours worrying over the peril of his dear Master?

"How can I prepare for what as yet I know nothing about?" asked Apollonius in that strangely disconcerting direct way of his.

Damis opened his eyes in hopeless perplexity. Would he never understand the old man? "Do you mean to say you are going to argue a cause which involves your own life, without any kind of preparation?" he asked.

"Certainly I do. All my life has been passed without preparation until now, without fixed plans, and so it shall be to the last." Then he appeased Damis by showing him his little joke, if it may be called that. For he told him how Phraotes had taught him how to tame lions–a queer occupation for a philosopher, especially one who had quite recently argued a rich, ignorant young man out of his ignoble occupation of teaching birds to talk with a cockney accent, or whatever corresponded to cockneyism in the days of Domitian and the Roman 'Arrius, and to spend his time learning to speak decently himself. *Tyrants are lions*, said the Master, and Phraotes was really telling me how to deal with tyrants, not too severely, and not too gently.

LESSON FROM AESOP

"In Aesop there is a fable of a lion who lay stretched out in his den, not sick, but only pretending to be so, for the purpose of seizing on every animal who came to see him. But Aesop adds there was a fox, who in considering the case of this lion observed: 'I do not find that anyone remains with him, nor the footsteps of any who return from him.' And yet," said Apollonius, "I should have thought more of the wisdom of the fox had he entered the cave without suffering himself to be taken; and on his return had been able to show his own footsteps."

He turned over and went to sleep, leaving Damis to think it out. Many of the Master's best lessons were garbed in the simplest form and after all, Aesop's fables were a divine gift of Mercury, Wisdom, himself. Could the old man really mean that though there were no footsteps that ever came back from the judgment–seat of that greater Nero, the awful Domitian, there was now a fox that would show the world how it might be done? The thought was too good to be true. Oh, if it were all over!

When it was day, Apollonius paid his adorations to the rising sun as well as he could in prison, and spoke to all who wished to hear him. About noon an officer came to prepare him for the audience.

"I'm ready, let us go!" said Apollonius on the instant, eager to be away. *He* was always dressed! Surrounded by four guards who kept at a greater distance than usual when guarding a common prisoner, he left the prison. In the background there was a figure that followed with fear and trembling and much sadness. Nobody noticed that inconspicuously clad man, for he was dressed much as the crowd were dressed; had not the Master told Damis not to make himself look peculiar?

But that other figure of Apollonius between the four soldiers how people stared! See, they keep their distance; he is an important one, that! But what a strange garb for such a man, look at the cut and fashion of it! Not a tailor in Rome but would lose every customer if he acknowledged having made it; linen, too. And look at his shoes, made of some kind of tree–bark or bast. What long hair for so old a man—must be ninety–five at least! Surely he might show the Emperor the compliment of combing it, like Leonidas and his Spartans when the hosts of Persia came down upon them. It is the sign of a freeman to wear long hair, but a freeman need not neglect it; didn't they answer the Persian summons to surrender by saying to the ambassador: "they were combing their hair," and not a word more? "For me, I think he will soon have it combed for him, and perhaps a little more, too..."

The usual crowd–wit and levity. But very few felt quite like that this noon. There was something squalid in his garb, but there was something divine in his face and bearing; the latter was as superior to their own natures, and they felt it, as their smart clothes were superior to his linen garment. There was a more serious current to talk and thought that ran through that Roman crowd that day. Even his enemies were overwhelmed with admiration at this old man who was yet an old man twenty years before, and might well have earned the right to live out his years in peace; but he had done what no man had ever done before or was ever likely to do again—he had actually come of his own free will to Rome to save his friends Nerva and Orfitus and Rufus! The thing was a prodigy to be spoken of in history while the world should last. They dared not whisper that Nerva was to be Emperor after Domitian, for so it had been foretold, or that others were for the other two of his companions, for the very stones in the street would turn informer, if they did; but they thought, they thought!

It was a busy scene. Throngs of sightseers eager to see and be seen. Great and small officials passing out of the palace with documents, and soldiers with their uniforms, friends and friends of their friends flattering those in office lest perchance they let fall crumbs from the imperial table; officials in the making going in; office–seekers elbowing them up the stairs; a prisoner under guard waiting to be tried; fashionable people greeting their friends and being greeted by them in turn with the gossip of the day; butchers and bakers and candlestick–makers jostling and chattering and gossiping, and all the traffic of a great city. Only one man in the midst of them seemed oblivious of it all; he was alone in the crowd as only a philosopher can be.

AT THE PALACE GATES

Now they had stopped at the palace–gates and Damis was able to creep a little nearer. He was very sad. Would he ever see his Master and Teacher again? True, this was not a trial; it was only a confrontation, but what was that to that devil Domitian, who was quite capable of killing the old man with his own hand at the first word of indiscretion. And who could trust Apollonius to say anything but what he chose to say? What was he thinking of?… A voice reached him from among the four guards; it was his Master speaking to him while they waited. Doubtless he appreciated his danger and his solemn situation, as Damis had long done.

"Looks to me like a public bath," said the old man. "Those who are inside are trying to get out, and those who are outside want to get in; the former have had their bath and the latter are yet un-washed!"

Damis was so taken aback at the comic suggestion that for a moment he forgot his sadness and depression, and actually smiled. Which was what Apollonius wanted him to do. Didn't he seem to hear one of the guards muttering: "it is a pretty hot bath you are in for this time, old man, no question about that!" or was it one of the passers–by, or only imagination?

Apollonius was absolutely unchanged. He chaffed Damis with looking like a dead man who thought the Imperial Palace was Hades, whose gates had all but closed on him.

Damis hardly laughed at this. "I do not feel like a dead man, not quite, but I do feel like one who is going to die, and that soon!" said Damis.

"I thought I had prepared you, Damis, to be always ready for death, like a true philosopher," said Apollonius. "Instead of that you do not seem to like it."

So they talked, and Apollonius drew the mind of Damis away from his troubles as they waited at the palace–gates. The guards wondered not a little at this strange old man who seemed to forget that the next few minutes might decide whether he was to be boiled in oil or have fishhooks stuck all over his back–actually the latter treatment was rumored abroad. And did not rumor recall that an old Jew visionary had undergone the oil treatment before what was left of him was banished to the islands–Patmos, or some place like that?

EIGHTEEN

PRISON

The Emperor finished the morning's business and went to the hall of Adonis after he had completed the sacrifice. He had not taken off the fillet of green leaves from his head and was still thinking of the sacrifice when Apollonius was brought in, Damis having been thrust aside at the gates. Suddenly the Emperor looked up from the flowers made of shells with which the hall was adorned, and for the moment he was more amazed than ever the Tyanean's friends had expected the latter to be. Aelian prepared himself for anything, especially the unexpected. How on earth could anyone say what would happen where Apollonius was concerned?

"You have brought me a spirit!" said Domitian to the Prefect, in amazement.

"Well now, I was just thinking you were like Diomed at Troy under the protection of Pallas, O Emperor," said Apollonius.–This was a promising beginning, Aelian thought, for did not Domitian consider himself specially protected by Pallas? But Apollonius continued: "She purged his mortal sight and gave him the power to distinguish between Gods and men. Now you show me that the goddess has not removed that mist from your eyes, for you would not have ranked men among the demons, if it were so."

"How long have you had your eyes purged?" asked Domitian.

"A good long while now, ever since I began to study philosophy."

"How is it you have come to consider the Gods as my greatest enemies?" said the Emperor.

"What, are you at war with Airchas and Phraotes the Indians, whom of all men I consider divine and deserving to be called gods?" said the Tyanean.

"Don't change the subject to Indians," said Domitian. "answer me as to Nerva, your intimate friend, and his accomplices!"

""Certainly. What is your command? Do you command me to plead his cause or not?"

"Yes, plead it;" said the Emperor. "*For he is already convicted of crime.* And are you not in conspiracy with him? That's what I want to know!"

Aelian heard Apollonius adopt a confidential, gossipy sort of tone, as if he did not care how much he said, if he could only gain the favor of the Emperor by telling everything.

"Listen," he said, "and I will tell you how far I am concerned in the matter. Why should I conceal the truth?"

Things were going splendidly for the Emperor, but for Apollonius, how could Aelian retain a glimmer of hope? Here was the old man going to give the whole case away. Oh, why had he not let some lawyer prime him with what to say! The Emperor leaned forward with his ears ready to catch every little secret, and some big ones, too, for were they not going to send Nerva and Orfitus and Rufus to their deaths?

Apollonius began. Could Aelian believe his ears?

"I know Nerva is one of the most moderate and mild of men. I know that he is much attached to you. He is an excellent magistrate, so little disposed to meddle in affairs of state that he even shrinks from the honors attending them. Besides this, his friends, Rufus and Orfitus, are in my opinion moderate men and despisers of worldly wealth; they are, in short, as far as I know them, men too backward to interfere where they ought, and where it is lawful. These are not the kind of men who seek to cause revolutions nor to help those who do."

Think of Aelian's feelings! He dare not show the slightest sign that he knew Apollonius and was secretly his friend. And now he dare not laugh. The Emperor was furious. He let go the vials of his wrath, saying anything and everything that came to mind and abusing Apollonius unmercifully, for recommending these disturbers of empire as good men.

"I know you all, you wicked ones! If I asked them about you, they would say you were neither an enchanter, nor hot–headed, nor a boaster, nor covetous, nor a despiser of the laws, because you are all in league together."

He had let out the whole arsenal of the accusation, and every arrow was blunt and every feather frayed. What a dossier! Still, what philosopher was ever accused otherwise? But there was one shaft left in the quiver.

"I know as well as if I had been on the spot with you," thundered the Emperor, "the oath you took, the place where you met, and the cause of your conspiracy. And I know the sacrifice you made."

That was a clincher. Apollonius was calm.

"It is not honest in you, O King, nor agreeable to law to enter into a judicial discussion of what you are already persuaded, nor to be persuaded of what has not been discussed. If such is your pleasure, permit me to begin my defense with saying that you are prejudiced against me, and are more unjust than the common informer. He at least promises to prove what you take for granted without proof."

Had anyone, *could* anyone, ever have spoken to Domitian like that before? There was no eluding the argument.

"Get your defense ready then," said the Emperor, "begin it in any way you like. As for me, I know where to begin and where to leave off."

Then his fury broke out afresh. He treated Apollonius like the worst of felons. His hair was to be cut off (the barber knew how to blunt his scissors and razors, and if they wouldn't cut, why what was to prevent those old locks being *pulled* out?); he was loaded with fetters and cast among the worst criminals in the prison.

"I do not think you need fear my hair," said Apollonius. "It is not very dangerous. But what is the good of binding me in chains if you think I am a magician, an enchanter?"

"I have bound you and will not let go until you change yourself to water, or a wild beast, or a tree."

"Supposing I could do even that, I would not, lest I should betray those men who run the risk of being put to death! What I am, that I will remain, subject to all you can inflict, till I have pleaded their cause."

"And who will defend yourself?" asked the Emperor.

"Time, the spirit of the gods, and the love of philosophy to which I have been devoted," said Apollonius.

There were secret enemies of Apollonius, and this kind of thing did not please them at all. So they did what such secret enemies have ever done. They spread abroad the report that he had made his defense and was condemned, and that is why he was shaved and put in irons. But this is obviously untrue, as Damis says, for if he was then condemned, why was a letter, a long prolix yarn spun in the Ionian dialect, which Apollonius never used except to make his will. In this he is made out a suppliant, as though he had confessed himself guilty. Was there ever a philosopher who went through the eternal program without these things; will there ever be one, or will the method of playing the game ever change? The hid hand behind was well known to Apollonius, as he showed when the next move on the board was made.

Two days later another visitor entered the prison and promised to help Apollonius. He was a Syracusan, a Sicilian, and he tried other tactics than the agent who had failed before. Apollonius knew he was an agent from the first and governed his conversation accordingly, giving the strangest and most unexpected philosophical replies to all the questions that were volleyed at him from the very beginning. That tack was no good.

155

"This time it is not a matter of Nerva and the others; as far as I understand, the Emperor pays no attention to those calumnies any more. The matter is much more serious, and the man who gave him the information about the present accusations of your treasonable language in Ionia is a man of no small reputation," went on this *mind and tongue* of Domitian, with subtle suggestion. "These things are so serious that the Emperor has forgotten the other things in his displeasure."

"I suppose the accuser you mean is someone who has won a crown at the Olympian games and now wants to win another for his skill in calumny," said Apollonius. "I know who he is. It is *Euphrates* who has libeled me; I am indebted to him for several kindnesses of the sort. He even went so far as to calumniate me to the gymnosophists of Egypt, and if I had not known about it beforehand I might have returned without ever seeing them!"

The Sicilian *agent provocateur* and spy was taken aback by this reasoning.

"What! Do you mean to say you think that was more serious than being accused by the Emperor–just the possibility of being underrated by the gymnosophists?"

"Certainly I do; for I went to them to obtain knowledge; but now I am come to impart it."

This amazing man!

"What have you come to communicate?" asked the informer.

"I have come to tell the Emperor I am honest and of good repute. He doesn't seem to know it yet!"

"I think it would be better to tell him now, what you refused to tell him before, if you are alive to your own interests," said the spy. "If you had only spoken when you had the chance, you would not now be in chains."

The cat was out of the bag. They were once more trying to get him to betray Nerva. But the wily philosopher met this underhandedness in the way philosophers do, always with success. He was just straightforward.

"Well now, you see me in chains because I told the Emperor the truth,"he said. "What do you think would be the result if I told him the contrary?"

The spy had had enough of it. He left Apollonius alone, saying as he went out, "This man is more than a philosopher!" He was right, as Damis found in a day or two.

They had many conversations, Damis sad and hopeless, Apollonius assuring him again and again that they should not be put to death. As well argue with the hangman that nothing was really going to happen.

Damis asked: "If you are going to be set at liberty, tell me when?"

Apollonius said: "Tomorrow, if it depended on the judge. But if it depended on me, this very minute!" So saying, he drew his leg out of its heavy fetters and said: "You see how free I am! So cheer up!"

THIS WAS NO VULGAR MAGIC.

For the first time in all these long, long years of daily intercourse, a great light began to dawn on Damis. For this old man, of well nigh a century of mortal years to his present count, was acting in a manner above the human, in a way divine. Without any sacrifice or prayers, or saying a word, he could do what others do not do with all the help of the gods, making a mockery of his fetters. Then he put his leg back and continued to behave "like a man in chains!"

Philostratus, perhaps, belonged to the same school of philosophy, for he wrote just a little more than a century later in collaboration with others at the wish of the Empress Julia Domna, who was also a student. Therefore, to avoid foolishness, he digresses to assure the reader that this was no vulgar magic, and to warn all young people to have nothing to do with 'magic' or magicians, and not to make themselves acquainted with their practices, even in merriment or sport. He knew the danger.

Then one day Apollonius was removed again to the larger room where, free of his fetters, he was able to meet the other prisoners again. They received him with joy, as children who receive their parents in love, after fearing they would never see him more. The Emperor in giving this concession gave out that he would be tried in five days' time. Apollonius never ceased advising and encouraging the prisoners, and though he knew it might not be needed, he wrote his defense; chiefly to have it on record what the accusations were and their refutation, it seems.

The next day, Apollonius called Damis and told him to go to Puteoli and salute Demetrius. "Better walk instead of going by boat," he said quietly; "you will find it the best way of traveling. Then when you have seen Demetrius, go down to the shore by Calypso's Isle and you will see me."

"What! Alive, or how?" exclaimed Damis.

Apollonius laughed. "Alive, in my opinion, but as one raised from the dead in yours," he said cheerfully.

So Damis went. He had learned what those quiet little asides of the Tyanean meant, and though a three days' tramp was more irksome than going by boat, he walked. Between hope and fear he went with torn emotions. Would his Master be saved? Would he be saved? The gods alone know.

Arrived at Puteoli he found there had been a fearful storm and many ships were wrecked. Then he knew why he had been bidden to walk.

NINETEEN

TRIAL

The day of the trial came, and from sunrise those of high rank in the Empire had access to the court. They report that the Emperor ate nothing from the preceding day, being preoccupied with the case. He read the indictment over and over, sometimes with fury and at other times with a certain degree of calmness.

Writing from the safety of a century later, Philostratus says we may assume that Domitian was highly incensed at the laws for ever having invented tribunals!

As usual, Apollonius seemed the least concerned in the matter. He argued wisely with the officer in charge, who approved what he said and was friendly.

Defense was by the clock. A time was set and the defense had to be completed in that period. There was no chance to talk out the case. Drop by drop the water in clepsydra told the passing of the seconds until the last drop had run out and with it the prisoner's right to speak.

"How much water do you want for your defense?" asked the officer.

"If the Emperor permits me to say as much as the cause demands, then all the water in the Tiber would not suffice," said the Tyanean. "But if only as much as I wish, then the amount will be regulated by the number of questions the accuser asks; I shall answer quickly enough."

"You have cultivated very opposite talents, I see," said the officer, "in being able to speak briefly or at length on the same subject."

Nothing worried Apollonius. He was as ready to debate the point as he was to think of his personal danger. "Hardly opposite," said he, "but if anything, rather similar, for he who excels in one will not be deficient in the other. But there is a talent between them, which rather than the third I should call the first talent of an oration; for it partakes of both. The fourth talent on a trial is what I call silence."

The Irish translator of Philostratus gives the officer's comment.

"Sure," returned the officer, "this is a talent which can be of no use, either to you or any other person in a capital information."

"And yet," said Apollonius, "it was extremely useful to Socrates, the Athenian, when he delivered himself from the charge brought against him."

"And pray," answered the officer, "how did it serve him, inasmuch as he died in consequence of being silent?"

"He did not die," said Apollonius, "but the Athenians believed it."

While they were waiting at the door of the tribunal, another officer came out and said: "Tyanean, you must enter naked!" This to an old gentleman well advanced in the nineties! After all, he was from one of the most important families of Cappadocia, of the Greek colony there.

"What, have you brought me for a bath, then? I thought it was to plead my cause!"

What would the old man say next? He did not seem a bit overawed.

"I am not thinking of your clothes," said the officer. "But the Emperor has given an order that you are not to bring with you any amulet or book or charm or any writing whatever." The informer and accuser had thus at a blow cut the prisoner off from his defense, for who can defend himself without his parchments and tablets?

Apollonius answered loudly enough for Euphrates to hear and for all the others: "Does he forbid me to bring a rod for the back of those who have given him such silly advice?"

Euphrates was terrified, or at least pretended to be so. He probably did not have to pretend very hard. "O Emperor!" he cried in alarm, "this conjurer threatens me with stripes as being the man who gave you this advice!"

Apollonius did not care if all Rome heard him. "If that is so," he said, "you are more of a conjurer than I am. For you confess you have persuaded the Emperor to believe I am what I could never persuade him I am not."

The point was neat, but it is hardly likely the officers and others in the court dared applaud, as they might have done in the presence of any other than Domitian.

All this time there stood by Euphrates a freedman of his who had been sent into Ionia with money to collect every morsel of tittle–tattle that could be brought against Apollonius. Any one who had the least little thing to accuse him of was to have whatever price he liked for the information. How could a man escape from such a black situation?

The court was packed, as if for some great event, with all the high officers of state. Domitian had determined to make the most of the case as one of rebellion. Damis was not handy; he had gone tramping to Puteoli, three days on the roads; or Apollonius would likely enough have been discussing with him the respective merits of Babylonian and Egyptian music, or telling him about the playful megalosaurus that once disported its huge bulk in the mud, or discoursing on the happiness that ever springs up spontaneously in the heart of the true philosopher, or the giants that dwelt in the earth 'in those days,' or anything really interesting like that, to relieve the boredom the court caused him, as if his life were a matter of no particular interest to anyone. But as no Damis was there, he looked around him nonchalantly and never noticed the Emperor at all.

Never even saw him! And that after all Aelian's telling him not to show disrespect! Poor Aelian!

The accusing attorney, Euphrates, saw his chance and seized it. "I command you to look upon the Emperor as the God of all men," he thundered.

Apollonius said not a word, but he made a characteristic gesture which he had often done before. He 'looked up'–and what could they not read in that philosophical look! It said as plain as a pikestaff: "O Jupiter above, is not the one who admits such gross flattery viler than the flatterer himself. Thou art the God and Father of all!"

The Emperor was probably boiling with rage, but in the presence of all those high officials and all that state pomp and the stake he was playing for, he held himself in. Aelian, without a doubt, was looking blue enough, but dared not show a sign of even recognizing the prisoner. Euphrates was beside himself with fury.

The Charges:

"O Emperor, measure out the water now, at once, before we are all suffocated with this fellow's talk." (Apollonius had not said a single word!) "I have here the roll of the heads of the charges he must answer, and reply distinctly to each and every one of them." The sting was in the tail. As the words rolled off his smooth tongue he was thinking of the last terrible charge. All the rest were mere pinpricks to enrage and tire the bull before finishing him, though they could be made to look ugly enough before Domitian. Actually the latter commended the accuser for his good advice and told Apollonius to plead as Euphrates should prescribe.

So all the articles of the accusation were at once cut down to four. The pinpricks could go, now the Emperor was won over publicly.

Question one was simple enough, just a sort of banderilla to get things started.

"Why do you not wear the same kind of clothes as other people, but only such as are peculiar and truly singular?"–Oh, the crime of being unfashionable, the turpitude of an old suit, the iniquity of a last year's frock!

"Because the earth which supplies me with food, supplies me also with raiment, and by wearing garments derived from it, I offer no injury to miserable animals." Apollonius was brevity itself in his reply.

"Why do men call you a God?"

"Because every good man is entitled to be so called!" said Apollonius. He had not forgotten Iarchas and the Indians.

Question three. Things were getting a little warmer!

"How did you come to predict the plague at Ephesus? Was it by an instinctive impulse or by mere conjecture?"

"By living on a lighter diet than other men, O Emperor, I was the first to see its approach. Now if it meets your approbation I will enumerate the several causes of pestilential diseases."

Domitian pricked up his ears. He saw the coming argument this irrepressible old Cappadocian Greek was going to spring on him, *on him*, the Emperor! "It is not necessary to go into that now," he said. –And well he might, for he knew the old man was as likely as not to say that the injustice of rulers, emperors for instance, *Roman* emperors, was such a cause. To say nothing of a Roman Emperor who had killed his brother Titus and then married his daughter, his own niece Julia, after first going through the little formality of putting her husband Sabinus (who was a relative of his own) to death! Had they not deliberately omitted from the dossier the serious accusation that when the Ephesians offered a sacrifice to the gods for the averting of such evil consequence as this ghastly crime could not fail to bring, Apollonius had been heard to mutter in none too low a voice, "O night of the Danaids, how singular thou hast been!" The Danaids had stabbed each one her murderous husband rather than accept him, but Julia never even offered to scratch her uncle Domitian with a buckle–pin! Why had not that ass of a Euphrates foreseen this and avoided giving the naked old nonogenarian such an opening? Domitian began to have his doubts of Euphrates after all had seemed so cunningly and infallibly arranged. Well, there was the fourth question. That will do the trick and rid us of this turbulent philosopher. Sacrificing a boy at midnight by moonlight to see what no mere old wives' almanac could foretell, his own death and the identity of his successor—that was a crime if you like, and proved up to the hilt! The informer had *seen* Apollonius and Nerva doing it; he was in the very same field at the time.

But what was the accuser up to? The eager court expected him to break out into a furious onslaught that all the wisdom of all the Apolloniuses in Rome could not withstand. Instead, he stood pensive and thoughtful. Was he going to spring a cunning lawyer–like trap just when all thought he was embarrassed? No, he seemed to be approaching the question on a sort of gentle gradient.

"Apollonius, tell me on whose account you sacrificed a boy on the day you left your house and went into the country?"

Now if Damis had been named Sam Weller, and if he had been in court, even he might have seen that this wonderful old philosopher was slowly turning the terrible trial for his life into as much of a joke as he ever turned all his troubles and dangers. Why not prove an alibi?

Apollonius spoke as to a naughty little child: "Speak nicely, please. If it can be proved I left the house on the day named, I will grant my being in the country and offering the sacrifice in question; more than that, if I did so sacrifice, I will allow that I committed the atrocity of eating the flesh on that occasion. Now while I admit this, I shall demand that persons both of credit and character substantiate the fact."

Checkmate! The whole court roared with applause such as that Imperial tribunal never knew before, right in front of Domitian, who was only doing it all to have a show of justice in condemning Nerva, Orfitus, Rufus, and Apollonius too. He had decided to kill them all anyway, and all this pomp and circumstance were merely to show that he could not possibly condemn a man without a fair trial. Now here was a queer fix. All the imperial officers in Rome, the elite of the empire, assembled to see his 'justice,' were witnesses that his accusations were all moonshine. Even Domitian was sharp enough to see the force and ingenuity of the naked old man's defense and he did what even Domitian could not avoid doing. He gave his judgment.

ACQUITTAL

"Apollonius, I acquit you of all the crimes laid to your charge, but you shall not go until I have had some private talk with you."

Did ever a *cause célèbre* end so wonderfully? What a gossiping there would be in Rome that evening! What a newsbearing throughout the Empire and beyond the borders! It was worth living in these modern times to have been present at such a trial. How the state officials and grandees of Rome would picture to themselves the great story they would tell their grandchildren, of how they saw the famous Apollonius tried and acquitted by the butcher who never acquitted anyone unless he had to. Ah, but he is speaking again; let us hear every word.

"O King! I thank you for this," said the even tones of Apollonius. "But on account of the wicked informers who infest your court, I must tell you your cities are in ruins, the islands are full of exiles, the mainland echoes with groans, the army is shaken with fears and the senate undermined with suspicions. Listen to me, I beg you, and if you will not, send persons to take my body, for it is impossible to take my soul. I will say more, you cannot even take my body, for as Homer says, 'not even thy deadly spear can slay me, because I am not mortal."

In uttering these words he vanished from the tribunal, "taking the wisest part, as I think," says the dry comment of Philostratus, "when all the circumstances are considered, for it is notorious that the Emperor was insincere and bore him no good will!…"*

And that is how he "passed through the midst of them without being seen."

*See Appendix II.

165

He had promised, you see, that he would stay in the Emperor's power until Nerva and his friends were no longer in danger. And he had kept his word.

Damis carefully preserved the long speech prepared for the defense according to the time allowed by the water–clock, though with the refusal to let Apollonius take even a scrap of writing with him and by limiting him to four questions only it had to remain undelivered.

TWENTY

Freedom, 'Resurrection' and on to Greece

After Apollonius had departed from the tribunal the Emperor behaved like one under a divine influence, and in a way not easy to be explained, because it was totally different from the general expectation of those who were best acquainted with him. They expected him to burst out into violent exclamations, and to have issued orders throughout the whole empire to discover and prosecute Apollonius wherever found. But whatever the cause, the event was the very reverse and he did nothing in the matter.

He even heard another case the same day in regard to a will. Domitian not only forgot the names of the parties but the arguments used in the case while it was proceeding. He asked meaningless questions and gave answers that had no bearing on the case. But the flatterers around him made him believe that nothing had escaped his recollection.

All this happened before midday.

Damis had arrived at Puteoli the day before and had told Demetrius all that had happened to the moment of his leaving Rome. Damis ought not to have feared and it was unworthy of a philosopher such as Demetrius to have doubts, but both of them were uneasy enough about Apollonius. They wanted to do as he had told them, but they knew they would never see him again, for who ever escaped from Domitian?

They walked by the shore near Calypso's Isle as he had told them, but their hearts were very heavy. They rested in a nymphaeum where statues of nymphs surrounded a pool bordered with white marble. They talked of the water which never overflowed and never diminished when drawn from. But they failed to make any show of interest and got to talking of the last hours of Damis with the master.

Damis could hold his grief in no longer. He cried aloud in an agony of grief: "Oh Gods, are we never more to see our good and valiant friend?"

"You shall see him, or rather you *have* seen him," said the beloved voice of their dear Teacher, the peerless philosopher of Tyana.

"What, alive?" said Demetrius, carried out of himself. "If he is dead we shall never cease lamenting him."

Apollonius stretched out his hand and said: "Take it, and if I escape you, regard me as an apparition just arrived from the kingdom of Proserpine, like those which the terrestrial gods present to the eyes of afflicted mortals. But if I bear being touched, I wish you would persuade Damis to think I am alive, *and have not yet laid aside the body.*"

Demetrius and the doubting Damis doubted no longer, but ran to him and kissed him. After a while they asked if he had made any defense. In their forlorn talk they had argued, *anything* to keep down the gnawing grief of their hearts. Demetrius had thought he had made no defense because he knew he must die, though innocent. Damis thought he had made one, but sooner than expected. But neither of them thought he had made it that very day, a few hours before, *in Rome*, at a distance of three days' journey!

"My friends, I have made a defense," he said. "I did so a few hours ago, and we are victorious. That was just on noon."

"How have you made so long a journey in so short a time?" asked Demetrius.

"Think what you like about it," he replied. "But do not imagine I made use of the ram of Phryxus, nor the wings of Daedalus. Put it down to a God."

Damis remembered how he had said "he was going on a very strange journey" and they had wondered if he meant he was going to some far country on the arrow of Abaris the Hyperborean, who made the circuit of the earth on an arrow, without food, or any fanciful explanation but the right one, that he was going to Rome to face the Emperor.

Demetrius asked a hundred questions about the trial, for he said he could see that a God was interested in all Apollonius did or said and made his every action prosper. He wanted to hear every detail to tell Telesinus, who a fortnight before had dreamed he saw a river of fire overwhelming everything except Apollonius who passed through it safely, dividing to give him passage. Telesinus knew it was a joyous omen.

"I am not surprised that Telesinus should think of me in his dream," said Apollonius, "for I know he has long thought of me when awake." Then on the way to the city he told them all about the trial.

Then they were in the depths of despair once more. There was no manner of doubt that the Emperor would send all over the Empire for him and capture him somehow. But he calmed their fears, and even Damis said he was at last convinced there was something exceptional, something divine about him, and that it would be all right in the end if he said so. He told Demetrius about the unfettered leg in the prison as the incident that had made him think there was something superior in the wisdom of Apollonius. So they agreed, since it was evening–time, to go to the nearest tavern and care for their beloved master. But he said he needed nothing more than sleep, which he promptly took, after repeating some verses of Homer in place of his evening hymn. But he insisted that they should have a good meal.

169

LEAVES FOR GREECE

In the morning Demetrius went to ask what Apollonius was going to do. He could hear in imagination the hoof–beats of the horses sent posthaste with swift riders to take the Tyanean–he hardly dared look out on the road to Rome. But Apollonius again assured him that none should follow him where he went. The next thing was to go to Greece. Did Damis know of a vessel?

"We are at the sea," said Damis. "The crier is at the door, and I hear the shouting of the sailors and the noise of the anchor as they prepare to weigh."

"We will go in her to Sicily, and then to the Peloponnesus," said Apollonius.

Then they took leave of Demetrius, who was sorrowful at their going. But they bid him be of good cheer and keep up his courage as a man who has the interests of his friends at heart. So they set sail with a fair wind and came to Sicily. Oh! the sorrow of that day for the brave old Demetrius! The sorrow and sadness of farewell.

Rumor said in Greece that Apollonius had been burnt alive; he was alive, but had his back stuck full of little hooks; he was cast into a deep pit; he was drowned in a well. All these might be true. The only thing humanly certain was that his end had come. Even the suggestion that he was alive under perpetual torture seemed extravagant. How was it possible that he or anyone else could escape the homicidal clutches of Domitian?

Then, 'a voice ran,' a little undercurrent, a murmur, a rumor, a buzzing of tongues that grew to a torrent of passionate assertion passed through Greece that he was not only alive and well but no farther away than the temple at Olympia! It was incredible, but it was true.

All Greece flocked to the Olympic Games; they were the world's festival, unrivaled and unchallenged as an attraction. But now the whole country flocked to Olympia, from Elis, and Sparta, and Corinth. Athens was not in their territory, but the flower and cream of Athens came to the temple for the chance of a sight, a word of Apollonius. All the world went to Athens to college, Boeotians, Argives, Thessalians, people from Phocis, and undergraduates from all the known world. These joined in the exodus to Olympia, whether they had seen him before or not. Those who had not heard him thought it shame not to have done so; those who had, wished to extend their knowledge, if even by a crumb, a golden word from his divine lips. Even the magicians came, those who degrade divine things for money.

They asked him how he escaped. The old man's reply was very modest.

"I pleaded my cause and came off safe." That was all he said.

Which only made matters the more intense. For when those who now came from Italy told the truth and the wonder of that most wonderful trial at Rome, the people of Greece proceeded almost to the point of adoration. His modesty and refusal to exalt himself above others was a powerful proof of his really divine quality. The priests needed no proof. Had they not seen him in their holy of holies? It was not for them to explain their household affairs to the public, but one thing was absolutely certain, that Apollonius never took one penny for his teachings. Still, there were personal funds ever at his disposition. All the treasures of Babylon he had rejected except a bit of bread and onion "which make an excellent repast." All the treasures of Vespasian and Rome were naught to him; and Damis found their funds mighty low – the purse he carried was no great burden on their journey.

He told his old Teacher and Master. "I will remedy it tomorrow," said the latter. Damis said no more. *He* had said it was all right, and so it would be.

Next day Apollonius entered the temple and asked the priest for a thousand drachmas out of the treasury, "if the God would not think such a sum displeasing."

"A thousand drachmas! It is a matter of no consequence to the God; but I fear he will be displeased that you ask for such a trifle instead of more!" And the priest gave it to him.

Apollonius stayed forty days at Olympia after his 'resurrection,' (for the people thought it was little less than that), explaining a variety of matters with great wisdom. Then he departed to converse with Trophonius, whose temple he had formerly visited, though without seeing the God. But he promised to return and discourse in the towns, and assemblies, "in your sacred processions, mysteries, and sacrifices, and libations, for all these things require the assistance and advice of a good man." Thus he left for Arcadia attended by his real admirers, of whom not one was left behind.

The oracle of Trophonius was a peculiar one. It was consulted by entering a narrow underground cave, much resembling the entrance to the Inferno of the later Dante. The priests refused to allow Apollonius to go down as it was only for the wicked and impure to consult the oracle, not such as he. This oracle was the only one that spoke direct to the suppliant without answers passing through any intermediary. This Trophonius was a son of Apollo.

Refused entrance by the priests, Apollonius sat down and discoursed of the oracle and the manner of consulting it. Those who entered the cave went down in a crouching position, clad in white garments and holding cakes of honey in the hand to appease the serpents that might be in the cave. After consulting the oracle they emerged, some in one place and some in another at a greater distance. The whole place and ceremony appeared like some labyrinthine mysteries of the after–life of the dead. But Apollonius had little use for such mysteries; rather it might be said, in modern terms, that he himself was capable of preaching to and instructing the dead.

At evening–time he wrapped his cloak about him and prepared to descend. The God himself was so pleased with his conduct that he rebuked the priests for their treatment of Apollonius and ordered them to expect his reappearance at Aulis. Here they waited seven days, and at the end of that time Apollonius reappeared by a way untrodden by any before who had ever consulted the oracle. And with him he brought a little book, like the Sibylline oracles, "fitted for answering all questions." He had asked Trophonius what philosophy he considered most pure, and the book contained the opinions of Pythagoras, to which the oracle gave full approval.

"This book is kept at Antium, which on this account, is visited by the curious traveler," says Philostratus a hundred years later. "It was carried to the Emperor Hadrian along with some letters written by Apollonius (for all did not reach him), and was left in his palace at Antium."

All his followers, whom the Greeks named Apollonians, came to him out of Ionia, and with them the young men from the country round about, a vast multitude full of philosophical zeal and worthy of admiration. Great crowds went to hear the philosophy of Apollonius, which fell from his lips like the wealth of Gyges and Croesus, free to all who asked. He spoke from the heart and the Apollonians paid little or no attention to the professional rhetoricians.

He would not allow his young men to accept magisterial offices, nor would he let them have anything to do with lawyers, but drove away his flock when he saw them approach: "I do it through fear of the wolves coming and attacking the fold," he said, in the imagery of the prophet Enoch. Some thought this was because he had seen such bitter suffering, privations, and death in the Roman prisons arising out of the wranglings of the lawyers who fattened on the misfortunes of others.

Two years he stayed in Greece and then sailed into Ionia with his whole company. He philosophized at Smyrna and Ephesus, not overlooking other towns, and everywhere he was received worthily.

TWENTY ONE

Wisdom

The time approached when the gods had decided to deprive Domitian of the Empire. He had put to death Clemens, a man of consular rank, to whom he had given his sister in marriage. He proposed, three or four days later, that she should follow her husband.

Now there had been of late a strange phenomenon in the heavens. A corona, or circle, like a rainbow, had surrounded the sun and cut off its rays. Many talked of this corona (*stephanos* in Greek) and some feared that the world was coming to an end. But Apollonius resisted all attempts to get him to declare the omen. All he said was: "Keep up your spirits, for some light will arise out of this night."

Now Stephanos, a freedman of Domitian's sister, the wife of Clemens, brooded on the coincidence of the character of the phenomenon and of his own name. Now that his mistress was marked out for death he took a horrible determination. In the manner of the ancient Athenians he fastened a dagger under his left arm and then tied the arm in a sling, as if broken.

As Domitian was coming from the tribunal he approached and said: "O Emperor, I have matters of great importance to communicate."

Domitian lived by his spies and informers, who each mistrusted the other. What more natural then that he should welcome the disclosure of some new plot by a man who evidently feared a less direct method of communication. Besides, he was the freedman of his own sister. So he took Stephanos into his private room alone.

"Your mortal enemy Clemens is not dead as you think," was the startling message. "He is living in a place I know of, and is preparing to attack you."

Domitian, superstitious as he ever was, even in the smallest things, uttered a shriek of surprise and fear.

Then Stephanos struck him with the dagger in the thigh. The wound was mortal but it did not kill him instantly. Domitian was physically robust and not more than forty years old, and wounded as he was, threw Stephanos to the floor, where he stood over him and tried to tear out his eyes while striking him in the face with a golden chalice as he shrieked out to Pallas for help. This was in a room where sacrifices were made and the chalice stood by the altar.

The bodyguards rushed in, and seeing that the tyrant was losing strength, they put an end to his life.

This happened at Rome while Apollonius was at Ephesus in the year 96 A.D., or about the year 99 of Apollonius.

The aged centenarian was walking in the groves of Ephesus about noon discussing philosophical problems with inquirers or disciples. Something seemed to interrupt his train of thought and his voice fell; he appeared to be in a peculiar mood. He talked still, but mechanically and in a low voice; it was as though he were preoccupied with some other matter than that of which he spoke; then he became quite silent, losing the thread of his discourse. In this mood he often used to fix his eyes on the earth, as at other times he used to raise them with a meaning gesture. Suddenly he advanced three or four steps and shouted. He did this not as one who saw a vision but as though he were present at the scene.

This was no midnight imagining, but a noonday scene in the most popular resort of Ephesus. All Ephesus was there to catch if possible some grain of the wisdom that fell from the lips of the wonderful old seer who was reaching his hundredth year of the most perfect purity of life.

The vast crowd fell silent. Apollonius now was still, every sense alert as though watching some contest of which the issue was yet in doubt. Suddenly he moved with a gesture.

"Men of Ephesus!" he cried. "This day the tyrant is killed! This day, do I say? Nay, this very moment, while the words are on my lips. I swear it by Minerva!" He said no more. But it was a serious matter; for had he not sworn by Minerva?

Many thought him mad, yet they would have liked to think that what he said was true.

"I am not surprised you hesitate to believe a thing that is not even yet known in Rome itself, at least not everywhere. Ah! now, now they know; it has run through the whole city. Thousands believe it and are leaping with joy. Now twice as many know it, now four times as many—now all Rome knows it! Soon the news will be here in Ephesus. You will not do wrong if you suspend all sacrifices until the messenger comes. As for me, I will go and pay my vows to the gods for what I have seen with my own eyes!"

Was ever a more extraordinary noonday wonder witnessed in Ephesus! Messengers came and confirmed to a second every detail. Thirty days later Nerva sent a letter saying he was Emperor by the counsels of the gods and of Apollonius, and he could better maintain the imperial dignity if only Apollonius would come to Rome and assist him to govern the world—that is what the request amounted to! And Apollonius was a vigorous old man of ninety–nine! So the answer sounded a little strange when Nerva read: "We shall both live together a very long time, in which we shall not govern others nor shall others govern us."

And so it was. Nerva reigned but sixteen months "in which time he established a character of the greatest moderation," before he passed to his long life beyond the gates of death.

But before that, Apollonius, wishing not to seem unmindful of so excellent a friend and so good a sovereign, wrote him another letter in no long time, giving him wise advice as to the governance of the Empire. When the letter was finished, he gave it to Damis and said: "The critical state of my affairs needs your assistance, Damis. The secrets in this letter are for the Emperor and are such as only I can communicate in person, or by you as a messenger." Well, Damis grieved to part with the old man, his dear Teacher and Master, even for so short a time as was needed to take a letter to Rome and return to Ephesus. But had he not learned to do as he was told, without cavil or delay? He took the letter, and Apollonius, seeing Damis sorrowful, remarked: "Whenever you are alone, and give up your whole mind to philosophy, think of me!"

In after years Damis often recalled the maxim of his old Teacher: "Conceal your life, and if you cannot do that, conceal your death."

He had done that. For the mission of Damis to the Emperor Nerva was of double purpose, and the second one was the one that concerned Damis most. It was that Apollonius might enter into his rest unseen and unwept by mortal eyes. Damis never saw him more.

Philostratus says that concerning the manner of his death, *if he did die*, various are the accounts. His wrinkles had something pleasing in them which added a brilliancy to his looks, which is "still (A.D. 210) to be seen in his effigy in the temple built to him at Tyana, and what literary monuments still survive speak more highly of his old age than they do of the youth of Alcibiades."

Philostratus traveled over most of the known world, and he never saw any tomb or cenotaph raised to Apollonius. But in all countries he met men who told wonderful things of him, and he adds: "Tyana is held sacred, not being under the jurisdiction of governors sent from Rome, and Emperors have not refused him the same honors paid to themselves."

When Aurelian took the town a natural reverence induced him to treat the countrymen of Apollonius the philosopher with lenience. The Emperor Hadrian made a collection of his letters, and Caracalla built a temple to him as a hero. Alexander Severus, who reigned after the book of Philostratus was published, had his statue in his private room.

Such was the life and passing of the Tyanean, best and greatest of philosophers.

Optimo Maximo: *"To the best and greatest."*

Appendix I

"The greatest teachers of divinity agree that nearly all ancient books were written symbolically and in a language intelligible only to the initiated. The biographical sketch of Apollonius of Tyana affords an example. As every Kabalist knows, it embraces the whole of the Hermetic philosophy, being a counterpart in many respects to the traditions left us of King Solomon. It reads like a fairy story, but, as in the case of the latter, sometimes facts and historical events are presented to the world under the colors of a fiction. The journey to India represents allegorically the trials of a neophyte. His long discourses with the Brâhmanas, their sage advice, and the dialogs with the Corinthian Menippus would, if interpreted, give the esoteric catechism. His visit to the empire of the wise men, and interview with their king, Iarchas, the oracle of Amphiaraus, explain symbolically many of the secret dogmas of Hermes. They would disclose, if understood, some of the most important secrets of nature. Éliphas Lévi points out the greatest resemblance which exists between King Iarchas and the fabulous Hiram, of whom Solomon procured the cedars of Lebanon and the gold of Ophir. We would like to know whether modern Masons, even 'Grand Lecturers' and the most intelligent craftsmen belonging to important lodges, understand who the *Hiram* is whose death they combine together to avenge?"–*H.P. Blavatsky, Isis Unveiled*, I, 19

It is always necessary to read H. P. Blavatsky's statements with care, if one would avoid misconception. The above remarks do not impugn the veracity of the historical narrative as given by Philostratus in 210 A.D., but they do show that the historicity is not the most important part, and that some of it is doubtless purely symbolical. But, as has often happened, very much history may be true as fact and yet used as allegory. Examples of such books will occur to every European.

"Jesus, Apollonius, and some of the apostles, had the power to cast out *devils*, by purifying the atmosphere *within* and *without* the patient, so as to force the unwelcome tenant to flight."–*Op. Cit., I, 356*

"No apostle, with the exception perhaps of healing by mesmeric power, has ever equaled Apollonius of Tyana; and the scandal created among the apostles by the miracle–doing Simon Magus, is too notorious to be repeated here again. 'How is it,' asks Justin Martyr, in evident dismay, 'how is it that the talismans of Apollonius (the *telesmata*) have power in certain members of creation, for they

179

prevent, *as we see*, the fury of the waves, and the violence of the winds, and the attacks of wild beasts; and whilst our Lord's miracles are preserved by tradition alone, those of Apollonius *are most numerous*, and actually manifested in present facts, so as to lead astray all beholders?" This perplexed martyr solves the problem by attributing very correctly the efficacy and potency of the charms used by Apollonius to his profound knowledge of the sympathies and antipathies (or repugnances) of nature."–*Op. Cit.*, II, 97

This passage occurs in a work "attributed to Justin Martyr." The unfledged curate, or whatever he should be called in those days, had to be fortified in his ignorance against people who *would* ask awkward questions and refused to be denied an answer. So we have a list of possible and probable posers and a considered reply that the young ecclesiastic may give to escape the dilemma. This was one of such questions, and it is not merely a hypothetical case but an actual statement of fact, requiring some explanation, if the ecclesiastical representative is to maintain that his system is the only one and the best and all others nowhere.

The statements are definite, not supposed, though the question may be. In all likelihood it had often enough been asked in actuality.

The author of the book of questions and answers states quite definitely that the talismans of Apollonius have power, that it is a visible fact that they prevent the fury of the waves, the violence of the winds, and the attacks of wild beasts. He states as a well–known fact that the "miracles" of Apollonius are most numerous and actually manifested as facts (which "are like pitchforks–you can't get away from them"). These are unrefuted statements. The insinuation that they *lead astray all beholders* means that they are mighty hard facts to whittle away so that the observer of them unreservedly accept the ecclesiastical dogma, and deny the truth or power of all religions except the new conglomerate that so loudly claims the whole field as its province. A suitable answer, as stated, is given, but it does not modify the facts in the slightest; it is calculated merely to soothe the insistent 'man at the meeting' who *will* ask difficult posers.

The 'Questions' are probably correctly *attributed* to Justin Martyr, since H. P. Blavatsky does not contradict, though the point is little more than a side issue. If the monkish zealots of the middle ages, as they did in many another case, found that the book was an awkward witness against them in their interminable discussions, and could not get rid of it, they would have reason enough to cast doubt on the authorship, this being a step towards casting doubt on the book itself. It is an old trick, similar to that of foisting upon the people the teachings that the 'apocrypha' (*secret* books–'books of the crypt'; *cryptographic* books, if you like) were '*doubtful* books,' as is taught in hundreds of schools today. When the trick is found out, it makes the discoverer curious to know why it was ever played, and if prompted to investigate, defeats its own object.

"Neither Iamblichus, Longinus, Proclus, nor Apollonius of Tyana, were ever mediums; for in such case they would not have been admitted to the Mysteries at all."–*Op. Cit., II, 118*

"Apollonius, a contemporary of Jesus of Nazareth, was like him, an enthusiastic founder of a new spiritual school. Perhaps less metaphysical and more practical than Jesus, less tender and perfect in his nature, he nevertheless inculcated the same quintessence of spirituality, and the same high moral truths. His great mistake was in confining them too closely to the higher classes of Society. While to the poor and the humble Jesus preached 'Peace on earth and good will to men,' Apollonius was the friend of kings, and moved with the aristocracy. He was born among the latter, and himself a man of wealth, while the 'Son of man,' representing the people, 'had not where to lay his head'; nevertheless, the two 'miracle–workers' exhibited striking similarity of purpose. Still earlier than Apollonius had appeared Simon Magus, called 'the great Power of God.' His 'miracles' are both made wonderful, more varied, and better attested than those either of the apostles or of the Galilean philosopher himself. Materialism denies the fact in both cases, but history affirms. Apollonius followed both; and how great and renowned were his miraculous works in comparison with those of the alleged founder of Christianity, as the kabalists claim, we have history again, and Justin Martyr, to corroborate.

"Like Buddha and Jesus, Apollonius was the uncompromising enemy of all outward show of piety, all display of useless religious ceremonies and hypocrisy. If, like the Christian Savior, the sage of Tyana had by preference sought the companionship of the poor and humble; and if instead of dying comfortably, at over one hundred years of age, he had been a voluntary martyr, proclaiming divine Truth from a cross, his blood might have proved as efficacious for the subsequent dissemination of spiritual doctrines as that of the Christian Messiah.

"The calumnies set afloat against Apollonius, were as numerous as they were false. So late as eighteen centuries after his death he was defamed by Bishop

APOLLONIUS OF TYANA

Douglas in his work against miracles. In this the Right Reverend bishop crushed himself against historical facts. If we study the question with a dispassionate mind, we shall soon perceive that the ethics of Gautama Buddha, Plato, Apollonius, Jesus, Ammonius Saccas, and his disciples, were all based on the same mystic philosophy; they all worshiped one God, whether they considered Him as the 'Father' of humanity, who lives in man as man lives in Him, or as the Incomprehensible Creative Principle; and that all led God–like lives."–*Op.Cit.*, II, 341–342

"The *Ineffable name*, in the search for which so many kabalists–unacquainted with any Oriental or even European adept–vainly consume their knowledge and lives, dwells latent in the heart of every man. This mirific name which, according to the most ancient oracles, 'rushes into the infinite worlds 'akoimhtw strofaliggi,' can be obtained in a twofold way: by regular initiation, and through the 'small voice' which Elijah heard in the cave of Horeb, the mount of God. And 'when Elijah heard it he wrapped his *face in his mantle* and stood in the entering of the cave. And behold there came *the* voice.'

"When Apollonius of Tyana desired to hear the 'small voice,' he used to wrap himself up entirely in a mantle of fine wool, on which he placed both his feet, after having performed certain magnetic passes, and pronounced not the 'name' but an invocation well known to every adept. Then he drew the mantle over his head and face, and his translucid or astral spirit was free. On ordinary occasions he wore wool no more than the priests of the temples."–*Op.Cit.*, II, 343–344

"The India of the early sages appears to have been the region at the sources of the Oxus and Jaxartes. Apollonius of Tyana crossed the Caucasus, or Hindû Kush, where he met with a king who directed him to the abode of the sages–perhaps the descendants of those whom Ammianus terms the 'Brachmans of Upper India,' and whom Hystaspes, the father of Darius (or more probably Darius Hystaspes himself) visited, and having been instructed by them, infused their rites and ideas into the Magian observances. This narrative about Apollonius seems to indicate Kashmir as the country which he visited, and the *Nâgas*–after their conversion to Buddhism–as his teachers. At this time Aryan India did not extend beyond the Punjâ."–*Op.Cit.*, II, 434

"Apollonius used no *darkened* room in which to perform his aethrobatic feats. Vanishing suddenly in the air before the eyes of Domitian and a whole crowd of witnesses (many thousands), he appeared an hour after in the grotto of Puteoli. But investigation would have shown that his physical body having become invisible by the concentration of *âkâsa* about it, he could walk off unperceived to some secure retreat in the neighborhood, and an hour after his astral form appear at Puteoli to his friends, and seem to be the man himself."–*Op.Cit.*, II, 597

"... after crossing the Hindû Kush, Apollonius had been directed by a king to the *abode of the Sages*, whose abode it may be to this day, by whom he was taught unsurpassed knowledge... At the end of his long and wonderful life he opened an estoeric school at Ephesus, and died aged almost one hundred years."– Theosophical Glossary, p. 27

Appendix II

"Apollonius of Tyana, the Greek, was probably as noble a character as was the Syrian Yeshua, or 'Jesus'. 'Jesus' is merely the Roman form of the name. We read of the marvels of Apollonius of Tyana, of his works and life, in the mystic "Life" written by Philostratus. But Apollonius is a *historical* character, and "Jesus" is not. The story of Apollonius is an interesting one. We read of his "vanishing away" before Domitian, when he was on trial before that eccentric and severe monarch, and much more..."–*G. de Purucker, Fundamentals of the Esoteric Philosophy*, pp. 221–22

There are close psychological similarities between these two wonder–cases (Jesus and Apollonius) of history; but they are not identically the same mystery."–*Op. cit.*, p. 237

"There are probably almost numberless cases where a Bodhisattva, a Buddhic ray, as the cycles of time pass, reaches out from the Lodge of our Masters, where the Great Initiator, the Highest One, is, the Man–Emanation of the Wondrous Being, and inspires and instills the Ancient Wisdom into the soul of some great and pure human being, such as was Jesus of Nazareth, and Apollonius of Tyana, and many, many others whose names are not familiar to us Westerners.–*Op. cit.*, p. 245

"A Nirmânakâya is a *state* assumed by or entered into by a Bodhisattva. When that state is ended the Nirmânakâya ends. *Kâya* means 'body', 'vehicle'. Therefore, Sankarâchârya, Krishna, Laotse, Jesus were Avatâras in differing degrees. There was a divine ray which came at the cyclic time of each such incarnation, and the connecting link, the flame of mind, was provided in each such case by a member of the Hierarchy of Compassion. But these Avatâras were not all equally great. Apollonius, while not an Avatâra, was a Nirmânakâya–a Bodhisattva;... the Bodhisattva stands actually, in the Hierarchy of Compassion, higher than an Avatâra, in the same way as a man who has gained divinity through his own efforts, and remains behind in the world of men out of compassion for it, and in order to help it spiritually, really stands higher than the devas or gods in their crystallized cold purity.–*Op. cit.*, p. 266

183

ABOUT THE AUTHOR

Malpas, Philip Alfred. Born February 24, 1875 at Birch, Essex (Stanway District) England, son of Joseph Malpas, an Anglican curate there, and Mary Menge. Little is known of his formative years, but his family background may have influenced his later researches. At age 18, he enlisted in H.M. Royal Navy, and was ship's clerk on a succession of 9 ships plying the world up to 1896. He then became assistant paymaster on 10 more until resigning his commission to the great regret of his captain on May 1, 1904. In that year, he met the Ponsonby family at Trinidad, showing them an album of photos of the Point Loma Theosophical Society, and soon after, the two Ponsonby girls enrolled there. He then joined the Point Loma Society and taught for the boys department in Horticulture and Nature Studies, and began his career of writing by frequent contributions to *The Century Path*, and later to *The Theosophical Path, and Raja Yoga Messenger* for children. Seeing his natural penchant for scholarly research, Katherine Tingley, leader of the Point Loma Theosophical Society, suggested he take up residence at the London Branch for serious studies at the British Museum. Accordingly in about 1910, Malpas began nearly 20 years of uninterrupted research and writing, with free run of the entire institution. He was supported primarily by the Branch Lodge until the financial difficulties of 1929 precluded his continuation there, and so moved to Essen, Germany as a private tutor in English, and lecturer. He is shown as a member of the Fremdspracheclub in 1931. At about this time he formed a small group interested in theosophical studies, including Mary Linné, and Emmi Haerter.

[These two woman were later jailed as enemies to Hitler's 3rd Reich for translating the entire *Secret Doctrine* into German, which manuscript was burned along with their personal library.] Malpas continued in Germany until 1939 when he was instrumental in helping several people of Jewish background defect to England. During the war, he was an instructor for Her Majesty's Forces at

London, and in 1946, Col. Conger invited him to Theosophical Headquarters which by then had moved to Covina, California. From 1946 to 1950 he was at Covina until Col. Conger's death when differences of opinion regarding leadership forced him to return to Germany. There, Mary Linné and Emmi Haerter were once again translating the *Secret Doctrine* into German, at Würtemberg. Malpas passed away there on July 22, 1958 at the age of 83.

His writings are voluminous, and only an overview can be attempted here. Of articles in Point Loma journals between 1900 and 1949, over 50 appear on every conceivable subject: some, such as 'Apollonius of Tyana,' 'St. Germain,' 'Cagliostro,' and 'Siddhartha Buddha,' extending over several issues. Theosophische Gesellschaft Unterlengenhardt has published his *Apollonius Von Tyana*, 1962. The following is a list of some of his unpublished manuscripts, most of which with commentary are translations from foreign language MSS. in the British Museum:

—*The Egyptian Mysteries and the Crate Repoa.*
—*Cagliostro's Masonry, and Egyptian Mysteries.*
—*Plato and the Esoteric Doctrine.*
—*Opus Tertium of Roger Bacon.* 368 pp.
—*Theosophists of Alexandria and Athens.* 750 pp.
—*The Mass and its Mysteries, by J.M. Ragon.* (tr. from Fr.) 250 pp.
—*Marcion, The Last of the Christians.* 119 pp.
—*Pistis Sophia, with notes by H.P.B. from Lucifer articles.* 188 pp.; 74 pp., 138 pp. Coptic text and diagrams inked in, charts, etc.

In addition, about 20 manuscripts dealing with early Christianity and its esoteric interpretation, and miscellaneous subjects exist, and should be worthy of publication in the future.